B. P. Pratten

A Dispassionate Enquiry Into the Causes of the Late Riots in London

In which the arcana of popery are candidly disclosed

B. P. Pratten

A Dispassionate Enquiry Into the Causes of the Late Riots in London
In which the arcana of popery are candidly disclosed

ISBN/EAN: 9783337244026

Printed in Europe, USA, Canada, Australia, Japan

Cover: Foto ©ninafisch / pixelio.de

More available books at **www.hansebooks.com**

A DISPASSIONATE ENQUIRY

INTO THE

CAUSE

OF THE LATE

RIOTS IN LONDON.

IN WHICH

The Arcana of Popery

Are candidly disclosed by

A PROTESTANT GENTLEMAN.

Nec tam pertinaces fore arbitror, ut clarissimum Solem sanis ac patentibus oculis videre se negent. LACTANT DE ORIG. ERR. LIB. II.

LONDON:

Printed for J. ALMON and J. DEBRETT, opposite Burlington-House, Piccadilly. 1781.

ERRATA.

Page 1, line 18, *palbably*, read *palpably*.
—— 35, l. 7, *lands Papists*, read *lands of Papists*.
—— 78, l. 11, *Didymns*, read *Didymus*.
—— 79, l. 10, *as any other seven*, read *as any of the other*.
—— 80, l. 3, *among Jews*, read *among the Jews*.
—— 101, l. 7, *are*, read *is*.

PUBLIC.

IT is self-evident that POPERY, as it exists in this country, is a grievous *national evil*, for it is either inimical to our laws and constitution, or it is not; if the first, then are the national prejudices against it, legal, constitutional, justifiable, commendable; and it is a *national evil* to support and tolerate in the heart of our country the avowed enemies of its laws and constitution; if the latter, then the laws, which make it felony and treason, are unjust laws; then the Legislature, to do justice, must contradict the law, and so bring upon our wise legislation the contempt and hatred of all mankind; those whom the law persecutes must, necessarily be for ever at variance with those whom the law protects. Thus the measure of *national evil*

evil is compleated by the exiſtence of unjuſt laws, which is the worſt ſort of tyranny, and the perpetual ſubſiſtance of enmity and hatred between his Majeſty's loyal ſubjects. Every man muſt allow, that at all times a *national evil* is to be removed; happy if at this time the removal of if it is within the power of the Legiſlature. Much has been ſaid upon the ſubject in Parliament, much out of Parliament, by the greateſt perſonages of the age, and to what effect? Popery is ſtill the ſame crime it ever was, and the national hatred of that crime perhaps more inveterate. The reaſon is obvious, the nature of the caſe has never been looked into; be it my humble theme to ſtate it. Let the Public read and judge, let the Legiſlature judge and *act*.

A DISPASSIONATE ENQUIRY, &c.

SUCH have been the late scenes of horror and confusion, that the minds of few persons in the nation have as yet regained that perfect calmness and security, without which, no judgment can be founded upon policy, truth or reason. And so universal has been the alarm, that the spirit of enquiry into the cause of the evil, can only have escaped those, who are divested of humanity, or void of the most common understanding.

It is not my purpose to fathom the depth of iniquity, which either planned or supported the late tumultuous insurrection. Were I a man of party, I could on one hand, with as much ease, connect a chain of circumstances, which would palpably convict the ministry of not preventing the evil, as I could on the other hand lay the rise and progress of it to the determined

termined efforts of Oppofition, to debilitate the reins of Government. I have attempted to trace each feparate effect from the fortuitous malice, and unconcerted motions of a fanatic rabble. I have alfo attempted to connect each feparate effect, and follow the direction of a premeditated deftructive principle, through all the wild efforts of frantic licentioufnefs. My fpeculations produced nothing more fatisfactory, than the probability of conjecture; and the mind which feeks conviction, will be fatisfied with nothing under certainty. Although the real caufe of thefe direful effects may ftill be, and for ever remain, a fecret impenetrable to the eyes of government, and of all honeft men, yet one truth is inconteftable, that the *oftenfible* caufe, which is known to all men, has produced the moft defperate efforts, which ever were attempted againft the conftitution and government of this, or any other country. The conclufion *ab actû ad potentiam* is univerfally admitted: and fo long as this caufe remains in all refpects the fame it now is, I fhall live in the daily expectations of beholding its effects breaking forth in frefh fcenes of horror.

A moderate independence in life has kept me out of the line of preferment, and an inclination to retirement has fecured me from every anxious purfuit of
ambition

ambition and avarice. I have ever cherished and gloried in the true spirit of patriotism, or real love of my country. At Oxford I was educated in the religion established by law; and I was early taught to entertain a less favourable opinion of the Roman Catholics, than of any other dissenters from the Church of England. I must however avow, that religion never was the favourite subject of my study, or researches. I supposed my own religion to be equally good with that of my neighbours, and freely own, that I seldom separated the ideas of bigotry and superstition, from the submission to the doctrine or adhesion to the observances of any religion whatsoever. I never ceased to entertain an awful deference for the Creator, and consequently could never suppose that he condescended to interfere with the actions of his creatures: I speculated much and often upon the laws and dictates of nature, and according to them did I square my conscience. I had not so much formally renounced, as imperceptibly lulled into oblivion the principle of Revelation. In this sort of security I rested, free from the grosser vices of mankind, (from which indeed want of inclination has chiefly preserved me) and assuming merit from rendering occasional services to my neighbours, and generally refraining from injuring any man.

B 2   I am

I am, perhaps, singular in having lived near forty years in this country without being personally acquainted with any one Roman Catholic, whom I knew to be of that persuasion, till the month of June, 1780. And it is also remarkable that the conversation never turned in my presence upon the subject of Popery, but I suddenly felt an indignation seize me against the superstitious bigotry and errors of that deluded sect. The ideas of Popery and ignorance, tyranny and cruelty, were always simultaneous: the early prejudices which I had imbibed in my youth against Popery, have occasionally broken out in sentiments and emotions, at which even humanity should blush. In fact, when I throw my reflection back upon my past life, I profess I can retrace no other religious influence under which I ever acted, than an unaccountable disgust and horror of Popery. I say unaccountable, for I ever gloried in my truly philosophic liberality, and unlimitted freedom of principle and action: and yet, to my confusion be it acknowledged, I never once thought of enquiring into the reason or cause of this prejudice.

From a long habit of retirement, I have for several years past seldom observed an effect, even of the slightest importance, but it has led me into the most diligent researches

researches for its cause. These researches have been frequently productive of conjectures and speculations, which the most serious consequences have but too fatally verified. I have hitherto suppressed them under the general conviction, that they would have shared the fate of Cassandra's Predictions, *Non unquam credita Teucris*. There are circumstances under which silence becomes criminal.

I was rouzed from my retirement by the excessive outrages of a mob assembled together, and acting under the sanctifying influence of *religion*. I was apprehensive that some mischief would ensue from the actual assemblage of so many thousands of the lowest class of the people. But like many of them, I thought the fury which might possibly burst out against the Papists, would be attended with little consequence or damage to the State. So forcibly did my early imbibed horrors of Popery then operate upon me. And the observation now naturally occurs to me, that if the intolerancy of Popery, considered as a religious prejudice, could so blind and mislead my judgment, who never took the interest of religion to heart, and who always endeavoured to refine my sentiments by philosophy; how much more forcibly must it have born upon those, whom the brutest ignorance could debase, and pulpit fanaticism mislead into the wildest excess excefs of bigotted phrenzy. The firft inftance of their outrageous fpirit, fo foftened my inveteracy againft the oftenfible objects of their fury, that I returned from the horrible fcenes of devaftation, which had been committed before my eyes, in the fanctuaries of two of the foreign Minifters, with a determined intention of fathoming to the bottom, that fpirit of enthufiafm, which had feized the minds of fo many thoufand men, and armed their fury againft their fellow fubjects.

It was nearly day-break before I had arrived at my own houfe on the morning of the third of June. Oppreffed with fatigue and amazement, I endeavoured to compofe my wondering thoughts to reft. It was in vain that I attempted it; I began to reafon with myfelf upon a fubject to which I never before had turned one ferious thought. My judgment was bewildered in proportion as I applied my thoughts to the fubject. I had feen the moft inhuman outrages fanctified by the cry of the religion, which I had ever profeffed, and fuppofed tolerant beyond any eftablifhment of the Chriftian world. The conclufion which alone I could deduce from all thefe thoughts and obfervations, was, that thefe outrages militated effentially againft the avowed principle, in which alone I had ever placed the perfection of all religion, which is, to do good to many, and evil to none.

none. I arose diffatisfied with myself, displeased with Popery, and shocked at the unbounded licentiousness of the mob.

I walked around my study, I cast my eyes along every shelf, but could fix neither eye or thought to any book, which I thought likely to develop the intricacy and contradiction into which I had worked my mind. I made an early visit to a neighbouring clergyman, in whose conversation I had often experienced much satisfaction and delight; he was a lettered man, of liberal and improved thought; he had spent the night in his usual uninterrupted tranquillity, and expressed his astonishment at the intelligence I brought him. I asked many questions, which I allowed him no time to answer. I poured upon him every observation which started into my mind. My words were inconsistent as my thoughts were bewildered. As I had frequently in former discourses with my reverend friend, reflected with great freedom upon the church, it may be easily supposed, that upon the present occasion, I was not tender of church, clergyman, or religion. I rouzed my friend to a degree of warmth, which he did not stifle; he concluded his discourse with assuring me, that the Church of England would soon have more to fear from Deistical Libertinism, than from the avowed opposition of Popery and the Devil. I took my leave of my reverend friend, and
attributed

attributed in part the unsatisfactory result of my visit to the unseasonable time of making it.

Under this embarrassment of thought, I stept into a neighbouring coffee house, where I beheld two gentlemen, who appeared to have spent the night as restless as myself; they were in eager scrutiny over the only morning paper, which had then come from the press. I seated myself on the opposite side of the room, and through fatigue and thought I closed my eyes, as though I meant to dose. Every thing was so quiet, that the lowest whisper of the two strangers distinctly reached my ear. It would be ungenerous to disclose to the world the particulars of a discourse overheard in this accidental manner, and the appearance I put on of sleeping, may possibly have betrayed them into a more unreserved freedom of expression. Suffice it to say, that they were both Roman Catholics whom curiosity, and concern had led to be spectators of the same nocturnal riots, of which I very accidentally had been also an eye witness. Their observations were to me entirely new, yet they were such, which naturally arose to them on the occasion, and I must now apologize to them for making public, even one of their many reflections. One of these gentlemen, after having resolved to emigrate from this devoted country, added very emphatically, Who can now stand

stand it? An innocent set of men have for ages groaned under a legal persecution, more rigorous than the very inquisition, and now to ease us of the severity of the law, the fury of every licentious fanatic acts upon us with impunity and exultation. Words cannot adequately express the emotions which arose in my breast at hearing this sort of insult. Their discourse was interrupted by the intervention of some other strangers; I returned home, turning in my thoughts what I had seen and heard.

As the discourse to which I had given such particular attention in the coffee-room, was the unconstrained and natural expression of sentiment and opinion upon a subject, to which I never before had had occasion of attending, I was the more amazed to hear a Roman Catholic coolly and steadily impute to the Church of England the *charge of intolerancy*, which I had ever looked upon as the essential characteristic of Popery. Reason and arguments, when used in an actual disputation, even with the utmost propriety, seldom convey any degree of conviction to the mind of the adverse disputant; each of them enters into the argument prepossessed against the opinion of his antagonist, and consequently against every thing, that can be alledged in support of it; it is far otherwise when we hear a subject discussed in an amicable conversation, in which we bear no part.

part. Had this same Roman Catholic asserted to me in discourse in the strongest manner, what I heard him coolly advance to his friend on the same subject, he would probably have effected no more than to rivet my prejudice against Popery the deeper.

The reception I had met with from my reverend friend, deterred me from applying to any other person for a solution of my present doubts; they harrassed my thoughts in proportion, as the subject was to me new, and the prospect of satisfaction appeared beyond the reach of my abilities. I attempted methodically to arrange my ideas. I resolved to commence my enquiry into the grounds and nature of Popery, by analyzing the essence of my own religion. We often learn the nature of one thing by its difference from another. Never was Chaos more confused, than what I soon fell into, by applying the test of philosophy to this, as I had to other subjects. The wildest inconsistency overwhelmed my intellects; my memory failed me, and the power of reasoning left me. The very grounds of my own religion, which the docility of youth had assented to, were now in the eye of the philosopher, absurdity, and contradiction. I left the pursuit with indignation, and again recalled to my mind the discourse of the two gentlemen in the coffee-room. Every principle of honour and philosophy was insulted

by

by this *charge of intolerancy*. Racks, tortures, and dungeons crowded my imagination, and all the horrors of the inquisition rouzed my indignation against Popery.

As my father had professed the law, by the practice of which he had much improved the family estate, a remote shelf in my study contained some remains of his professional library, in which the folio edition of the Statutes at large made the most respectable appearance. I had from my earliest youth contemned the servile drudgery of the law, as much as I afterwards despised the uncertainty and incomprehensibility of theology, and in fact, I had never opened a book which treated of either of these subjects since I had left the University. I had ever paid an almost implicit deference to the public acts of our wise legislature, and felt a gleam of satisfaction dawn upon my mind, as the idea arose of consulting the nation at large, by looking into the acts of their representatives. I waded with unremitting assiduity through many black lettered Penal Statutes against Popery, to the propriety of which, I could only square my mind by forcing back upon it every horror and prejudice, which I had before entertained of that crime. I endeavoured to convince myself (and for the time I in part succeeded) that Statutes so highly penal could never have been enacted, unless the objects of their rigour

rigour had exceeded the common lines of human malice and impiety. Weariness of mind and body called me to rest at an earlier than my usual hour.

During the restless hours which I spent upon my pillow, for agitation of mind prevented my sleep, I was lost in reasoning upon religion. In despite of the most plausible arguments, which nature and philosophy suggested, an unvoluntary conviction seized me, that I was fathoming a subject, to which the human intellect was absolutely inadequate. In the humiliation, into which this reflection threw me, I formed the resolution of attending the divine service in the morning; this was on Sunday the fourth of June. After what I have acknowledged, it would be useless to inform the public, that the church was not a place of my usual resort. I chose that church, where my before-mentioned reverend friend was to preach; though I had the precaution to place myself in a remote corner, which his eye could not possibly reach.

As it was in the sincerity of my heart, that I this day attended at church, not a word of the service escaped, even my critical attention. In the Litany I prayed the Lord with peculiar earnestness to deliver us, *from all sedition, privy-conspiracy and rebellion, from all false doctrine, heresy and schism;* in which words I included the whole evil of Popery.

Popery. The Epistle for the Sunday beginning with the words of Saint John, *Marvel not my brethren if the world hate you,* &c. raised in my breast a just detestation of that inexorable hatred, which I knew the Roman Catholics ever bore against all those, who were not of their own communion, whom they stiled heretics, infidels and unbelievers, and looked upon as objects devoted to eternal perdition. Nor was I a little flattered to find my reverend friend impressed with the same idea. He had chosen these very words for the text of his sermon; in which he displayed that emphatical energy and dignified eloquence, which precisely tallied with my ideas of pulpit oratory. After proving to the general conviction of the congregation, that Papists were all children of the man of sin, and the whore of Babylon, the spawn of the dragon, and the members of anti-christ; he displayed a voluminous catalogue of errors, crimes and impieties, of which he as clearly convicted the whole body of the Popish communion; and when he had excited in the hearts of his audience a full and thorough execration of Popery, as a distinctive character of the true church of Christ, he concluded with the last words of the same Epistle, *For hereby we know that he abideth in us, by the spirit, which he hath given us.*

From

From church I returned home, to compleat my search into the penal statutes against Papists; for I now found my mind much reconciled to the propriety and even exigency of such uncommon rigour. I had compleated this tedious examination towards the dusk of the evening, when I went to sup with an acquaintance at the east end of the town; as well to dissipate my thoughts, as to seek some relief, by disclosing them to a bosom friend. I was unfortunate in not finding him at home, but upon turning my back upon his house, I was alarmed by the cry of No Popery, at the end of the street in which he lived. I mixed with the crowd from curiosity; and heartily re-echoed the cry of No Popery; I soon found myself in Moorfields, for the mob bore down the streets such uncommon velocity. Here I beheld a renewal of the scenes, which had worked such an impression upon me on the Friday night; their operations appeared much more determined, and were regularly carried on without interruption or molestation, even under the eyes of the chief magistrate, and before the loaded musquets of the military. I must acknowledge that my own sense of humanity was on the present occasion almost deadened by my new acquired zeal for religion; in lieu of that spirit of philanthropy, which had freely acted upon me on the Friday evening, on a

similar

similar occasion, I was now endeavouring to drown the man in the guilt of the crime, for which I supposed him suffering. And if I may be allowed now to judge by analogy, from my own, of the feelings of others, the comportment of the chief magistrate, and of many even of the soldiery, who joined in the chears and huzzas of the mob, evidently demonstrates, that the guilt of the legal crimes perpetrated before their eyes (which they were officially bound to prevent and impede) had totally vanished, before the judgment, they had in their own minds passed upon the more guilty sufferers.

Notwithstanding all the efforts of my religious hatred of Popery, nature at last prevailed, and the savage outrages of the rioters awakened in my breast every sense of compassion and humanity: I returned home before the rioters had dispersed from this scene of depredation; and spent this as I had the foregoing nights in fruitless reasoning and unsatisfactory soliloquies. My sentiments were more distracted than ever. Philosophy, nature, and religion, alternately assumed the lead, and under their opposite directions, I remained in the very center of uncertainty, doubt, and confusion.

As my intention is merely to consider and disclose the nature of the *visible cause* of these direful effects, I am happy in having
a just

a juft reafon to draw a veil over them; they were in their nature fo extremely horrible, that the bare recollection of them is but too ftrong a memento to the public, to guard effectually againft every poffibility of their repetition. Individuals often run into errors and miftakes in affairs of the laft importance; but in my opinion, the public are infinitely more liable to that misfortune. I therefore entreat them not eafily to loofe the recollection of the confternation, into which this nation was lately thrown; be it remembered that one man, with the cry of No Popery, could affemble what multitudes he pleafed; and be it alfo frefh in the idea of every man, that while London was in the hourly dread of being confumed by fire, the cry of No Popery was the only fecurity of individuals. It is evident then, that Popery, as it now exifts in this country, has been the vifible caufe of all thefe late difafters. Be it not fuppofed that the temporary fubfiding of the violence has ftifled the fpirit which fomented the evil. The rehearfal of the Edinburgh Tragedy, improved on the London Theatre, is but too fatal a warning. Let the legiflature take into ferious deliberation that caufe, which has produced the evil: to me, nothing appears to have been lefs confidered. If the cool thoughts of an individual, fubmitted to the confideration of the public, and peculiarly

liarly of the present Parliament, can suggest and enforce the propriety of one measure of government, I shall think myself more than amply rewarded for the labour I have taken to investigate thoroughly the merits of a cause, which ever has, and ever will be productive of the most fatal consequences, in proportion as the nature of it is unknown, misunderstood, or misrepresented.

Never did I with such earnestness attempt to make a thorough and impartial enquiry into any subject as I have into this. And never before did I know the resistance of a stubborn, and almost innate prejudice. My mind, which in other pursuits had always exulted at the first dawn of truth, could in this refuse submission, when she appeared in her full meridian. I shall communicate to the public the result of my enquiries without any annotations or observations of my own. Let the reasons which could subdue the inveteracy of my prejudices, operate their own effect upon the minds of the candid public. For my own instruction I committed to paper the heads of the different penal statutes against Popery, as I read them over; and as they are known to few, who are not the unfortunate objects of their rigour, perhaps this sketch of them may not be unacceptable to some of my readers.

(*a*) The spiritual supremacy of the King was acknowledged and confirmed, and all spiritual subordination to the see of Rome was for ever abolished, and every degree of ecclesiastical or spiritual submission to the Pope was made punishable with all the penalties of a *Premunire*. (*b*) The King was afterwards more compleatly invested with the plenitude of all spiritual powers and jurisdictions. (*c*) And the first fruits and yearly tenths of all ecclesiastical livings were settled upon him as supreme head of the Church of England: (*d*) which emoluments were encreased by the suppression and seizure of all religious houses or monasteries, whose annual revenues did not exceed two hundred pounds. (*e*) Such effectual means were afterwards taken to establish more permanently the spiritual supremacy of the King, that it was made high treason to refuse the oath of supremacy when tendered. (*f*) In order to establish the spiritual supremacy with more dignity and solemnity, his Majesty was especially empowered to make bishops by letters patent and gave to his vicegerent in spirituals, Thomas Cromwell, a seat in parliament, with precedency before the Archbishop of Canterbury: (*g*) and to

(*a*) 24 Hen. 8. c. 12. (*b*) 25. Hen. 8. c. 20. (*c*) Ibid. c. 3. (*d*) 27. Hen. 8. c. 28. (*e*) 28. Hen. 8. c. 10. (*f*) 31. Hen. 8. c. 9. (*g*) 31 Hen. 8. c. 13.

compleat

complete the syſtem, his Majeſty was inveſted with the ſpoils and revenues of all the abbies, monaſteries, religious houſes, and communities throughout the kingdom. (*a*) And in the ſame ſeſſion of Parliament, the belief of tranſubſtantiation, communion under one kind, private maſs, auricular confeſſion, the celibacy of prieſts, and voluntary vows of perpetual chaſtity, was forced upon the nation under pain of death. (*b*) The capital puniſhments formerly inflicted upon incontinent prieſts, and of women offending with them, were ſoftened into forfeitures and other ſlighter penalties. (*c*) At laſt every innovation made in religion, from the year of the Lord 1540, every doctrine preached and maintained contrary to the King's inſtructions, ſpeaking irreverently of the holy ſacrament of the altar, and even reading the Bible in the vulgar tongue, were made crimes puniſhable with death.

(*d*) In the very firſt year of the next reign, every freedom of ſpeech concerning the bleſſed ſacrament of the altar, and particularly againſt receiving it under both kinds, was made puniſhable by arbitrary fine and impriſonment. (*e*) Then, every act which had paſſed under the late King,

---

(*a*) 31. Hen. 8. c. 14. (*b*) 32. Hen. 8 c. 10. (*c*) 34. and 35 Hen. 8. c. 1. (*d*) 1. Ed. 6. c. 1. (*e*) 1 Ed. 6. c. 12.

concerning doctrine and matter of religion was repealed, and the denial of the spiritual supremacy of the infant King, was made a crime of high treason, punishable with death. (*a*) The next step taken during the regency was to dissolve all colleges, chauntries, hospitals, fraternities, brotherhoods, guilds, and other promotions of the like nature, and confiscate the revenues upon which they subsisted to the crown. (*b*) Then an act was passed for a general change and uniformity of divine service, and the administration of the sacraments, throughout the realm; and the non-conformity thereto was made punishable with perpetual imprisonment. (*c*) A law was then enacted, that every person should observe fast on all Fridays and Saturdays, Embring Days, Lent, and some Vigils, under the penalty of forfeiting ten shillings for the first, and twenty shillings for the second offence; and imprisonment either for ten or twenty days accordingly, without tasting flesh meat during their confinement. (*d*) By another law it was strongly recommended to all priests to live single, but to prevent the danger of incontinency, they were allowed to marry. (*e*) Then all Popish books and images, whether carved

---

(*a*) 1 Ed. 6. c. xiv. (*b*) 2 and 3. Ed. 6. c. 1. (*c*) 3 and 4 Ed. 6. c. x. (*d*) 2 and 3 Ed. 6. c. 21. (*e*) 3 and 4 Ed. 6. c. x.

or painted, were ordered to be publicly burnt, defaced and destroyed. (*a*) His Majesty was afterwards impowered to appoint sixteen ecclesiastical, and sixteen lay commissioners, to change, alter, new model, and reform the whole system of religion. (*b*) Uniformity of divine service, and administration of the sacraments, was again enjoined under the penalty of perpetual imprisonment: (*c*) and several holy days and fasting days were appointed to be observed throughout the year, and the non-observance of them was made punishable at the discretion of the Spiritual Court; (*d*) and the issue of all priests and other religious persons, (notwithstanding their former vows of chastity and poverty) were declared legitimate and inheritable.

(*e*) The first act, which passed under Queen Mary, was to repeal every act which had made any offence felony, or in the case of Premunire, during the two preceding reigns: (*f*) and all the acts, which had passed during the same reigns, concerning doctrine and matter of religion, were also repealed. (*g*) The antient form of worship was re-established throughout the realm; and all persons maliciously disturbing and interrupting a priest, during the

---

(*a*) 3 and 4 Ed 6. c. xi. (*b*) 5 and 6 Ed c. 1. (*c*) 5 and 6 Ed. 6 c. 3. (*d*) 5 and 6 Ed. 6. c. xii. and xiii. (*e*) 1. Mar. c. 1. (*f*) 1. Mar. Sess. 2. c. 2. (*g*) 1. Mar. Sess. 2. c. iii.

divine service, or pulling down, defacing, spoiling, abusing, breaking or otherwise irreverently handling any crosses, chapels, or other repositories of the blessed sacrament of the altar, were declared punishable with three months imprisonment, and further until they should repent of their offence. (*a*) The Bishoprick of Durham, which had been dissolved by an act of her predecessor, was re-established; and the revenues, which were thereby vested in the crown, were restored to the Bishop and his successors. (*b*) After the Queen's intermarriage with King Philip, the several statutes made under Richard the Second, Henry the Fourth, and Henry the Fifth, concerning the suppression of Heresy and Lollardy, which had been repealed, were now revived. (*c*) An act was then passed to repeal every statute which had been made since the twentieth year of the reign of King Henry the Eighth, by which this kingdom had been disfranchized from the supremacy of the Pope; and the same act confirmed to the actual possessors, the lands of all abbies, monasteries, chantries, &c. which had been dissolved, during the two preceding reigns. (*d*) And finally, the

(*a*) 1 Mar. Sess. 3. c. 3. (*b*) 1 and 2 E. and M. c. vi. (*c*) 1 and 2 P. and M. c. viii. (*d*) 2 and 3. P. and M. c. iv.

church

church was acquitted and discharged in future, from all first fruits, yearly tenths, fifteenths, tithes, and other deductions, which during the two preceding reigns had been exacted by the Crown out of all ecclesiastical livings.

(*a*) The first Act passed under Queen Elizabeth, was to disfranchize once more the realm from the supremacy of Rome; and to restore to the Crown its spiritual supremacy and jurisdiction, by the repeal of several statutes made in the reign of the late Queen, and reviving others, which had passed in the reigns of Henry the Eighth and Edward the Sixth. An oath of acknowledgment of the Queen's spiritual supremacy was administered to every person, who received even the smallest profit, trust or honour from government, whether ecclecclesiastical or temporal; and the refusal was punished with perpetual disability to hold the same or the like in future: the maintenance of the Pope's or of any other spiritual authority over any part of this realm (excepting that of the Crown) was made a crime of High Treason, in its most extensive rigour. The right of Parliament was ascertained to interpret and adjudge, in all cases of religion, what was error, heresy or schism. (*b*) Another act was passed

(*a*) 1 El. c. i. (*b*) 1 El. c. ii.

to settle the uniformity of the divine service; and perpetual imprisonment was annexed to the speaking in derogation of the Book of Common Prayer. (*a*) Every person neglecting to frequent the church upon a holy day was amerced in twelve pence for every such offence, and made liable to all the rigour of ecclesiastical censure: the payment of first-fruits and yearly tenths to the Crown was again established, with some other additional charges out of ecclesiastical livings. (*b*) It was made High Treason to affirm that the Queen was a heretic, schismatic or infidel. (*c*) All persons giving or receiving absolution, according to the rites of the Church of Rome, or bringing into the realm, or having in their possession any agnus dei, crosses, pictures, beads, or such like vain and superstitious things; and all justices of the peace not disclosing an offence of this kind to them declared, were subject to the dangers, penalties and forfeitures of premunire. (*d*) All ecclesiastical persons were obliged to subscribe to the Thirty-nine Articles of the Protestant Religion, and upon their promotion to any ecclesiastical benefice or living, to make a solemn declaration in the church before the congregation, of their sincere and unreserved belief of each of them. (*e*) All persons either withdrawing

---

(*a*) 1 El. c. iv. (*b*) 13 El. c. i. (*c*) 13 El. c. ii. (*d*) 13 El. c. xii. (*e*) 23 El. c. i.

others, or withdrawn themselves to the Romish religion, with the aiders, maintainers, or concealers of any such persons, were made guilty of High Treason. (*a*) The forfeiture of two hundred marks, and one year's imprisonment, was made the penalty for saying mass; and the like term of imprisonment, with the forfeiture of one hundred marks, was made the penalty for hearing it; and the neglect of attending the divine service, according to the established form of worship, was punishable with the forfeiture of twenty pounds every month, and of two hundred pounds every year. All Jesuits and priests were ordered to depart out of the realm, and prohibited to come or return into it, under the penalty of High Treason; and it was made felony, without benefit of clergy, to receive or relieve a person of that description; every person contributing towards the support or maintenance of any such persons beyond the seas, incurred the danger and penalty of premunire. And all persons sending abroad a child or other person, without special licence, incurred the forfeiture of one hundred pounds for every such offence. It was also enacted, that every person not discovering a Jesuit or priest to a justice of the peace, should be arbitrarily fined and imprisoned,

(*a*) 25 El. c. ii.

prisoned, at the Queen's pleasure. (*a*) Every feoffment, gift, grant, conveyance, alienation, estate, lease, incumbrance and limitation of use of or out of lands, tenements or hereditaments, made since the beginning of the Queen's reign, or thereafter to be made, by any recusant, was declared void, as against the Queen's majesty, for or concerning the levying of pecuniary mulcts and forfeitures of such recusants: and the option was also submitted to her Majesty of seizing two-thirds of a recusant's lands, in lieu of the monthly forfeiture of twenty pounds for not frequenting the church. (*b*) Every Popish recusant was restrained under the pain of forfeiting all his life estate, both real and personal, to remove above five miles from his or her habitation, or usual place of abode. And in those cases where such offenders were not possessed of any estate in land not exceeding twenty marks annually, they were to abjure the realm, under all the rigour and penalties of felony.

(*c*) All the penal statutes, which had passed under Queen Elizabeth, were now most formally ratified and confirmed; and every person, of whatsoever age or sect, going abroad to receive a foreign education, forfeited his or her life estate, both real and

---

(*a*) 29 El. c. vi.   (*b*) 35 El. c. ii.   (*c*) 2 Jac. I. c. iv.

personal; and in order the more effectually to prevent the same, the officers of the port from which any woman or infant, under the age of twenty-one years, should sail beyond the seas, forfeited their places, with all their goods and chattels; the owner of such ship or vessel was made to forfeit it, with all its tackle; the master or mariner thereof incurred the forfeiture of all his goods and chattels, and was liable to be imprisoned for the space of one whole year. All teachers or keepers of private schools (being Popish recusants) incurred the forfeiture of forty shillings per diem, for the offence; as did also the maintainers or retainers of persons of this description. (*a*) An act was then passed to prohibit certain delicate meats from being sold in market, in Lent and upon fasting days, and for restraining licences to eat the same on prohibited days. (*b*) Several of the statutes of Queen Elizabeth were again confirmed; an oath of supremacy was ordered to be tendered to all persons (except the nobility) not under the age of eighteen years; several additional forfeitures were enacted to the crime of recusancy. A proclamation was framed against persons not frequenting the church; and if any persons against whom such proclamation should be made, did not make

---

(*a*) 2 Jac. I. c. xxix.   (*b*) 3 Jac. I. c. ii. and iv.

their appearance of record, at the next assizes or sessions, such persons were from thenceforth convicted in law of the crime, of which they were so indicted, and became liable to the forfeiture of twenty pounds by the month, or of two-thirds of their lands, without any further conviction. Every subject, either within or without this realm, reconciling another, or being reconciled himself to the church of Rome, was declared guilty of High Treason. And all persons having in their house, service, or pay, any recusants, were made to forfeit ten pounds every month for which they should so retain or maintain them. (a) Every informer of a mass said at any particular house or elsewhere, was entitled to one-third of the forfeitures of the persons so saying or assisting at it. No Popish recusant was permitted to come within ten miles of the Court, where the King or his heir apparent should actually be, under the forfeiture of one hundred pounds for every such offence. And every recusant convict, and also every person not having frequented the church within three months, was ordered to depart ten miles from London, under forfeiture of one hundred pounds (except tradesman having no other place of abode). No recusant convict was permitted

---

(a) 3 Jac. I. c. iv.

to practice the common law as counsellor, clerk, attorney, or solicitor; or the civil law as advocate or proctor; or to practice physic, or use the art or trade of an apothecary; or to be judge, minister, clerk or steward of or in any court, or to keep any court, or to be register or town-clerk, or other minister or officer in any court; or to be admitted even to the meanest employ, either military or naval, in the service of his country, under forfeiture of one hundred pounds for every such offence. Every married woman convicted of Popish recusancy, or not conforming within the first twelve months of her marriage, forfeited two-thirds of her jointure and dower, and was moreover disabled to be the executrix or administratix of her husband. Every Popish recusant convict was declared to be excommunicate, and was ordered to be treated as such. All Popish marriages and baptisms were prohibited, under the penalty of one hundred pounds, and burials of twenty pounds, for each offence. The life estates of persons, forfeiting the same for going beyond the seas, were to be enjoyed by the next of kin, who was no recusant, until such forfeiting person should conform to the established religion. Every Popish recusant was moreover disabled to present to any benefice with cure or without cure, prebend, or other ecclesiastical living, or to collate or nominate to any free school, hospital or donative whatsoever. All recusant convicts were disabled to be executors, administrators or guardians, not only to strangers, but even to their own children. The bringer from beyond seas, printer, seller, or buyer of any Popish books, incurred a forfeiture of forty shillings for every such book; and the justices of the peace were empowered to search the houses of recusant convicts for books, beads, relics, crucifixes, &c. and to burn and deface the same at the general quarter sessions; and likewise to search for and seize armour and ammunition belonging to them. (a) Receiving the sacrament, and subscribing to the oath of supremacy, was made the necessary qualification for naturalization or restoration in blood, by the reversal of an attainder. (b) The refusal of the oath of supremacy was again declared to incur a premunire, and disabled all persons so refusing it, to execute any public place of judicature, or to bear any other office within this realm; or to use or practice the common or civil law, or the science of physic or surgery, or the art of an apothecary, or any liberal science for gain, within this realm. Every married woman convicted of recusancy for not frequenting church, was

(a) 7 Jac. I. c. ii. (b) 7 Jac. I. c. vi.

condemned

condemned to imprisonment till she conformed, or until her husband chose to keep her at liberty, by paying ten pounds every month to the Crown, or by forfeiting two thirds of his lands.

(*a*) All persons convicted of giving or receiving a popish education abroad, or of sending others for that purpose beyond the sea, or of sending money or other support to any ecclesiastical or religious community beyond the seas, were made not only to forfeit their life estates both real and personal, but were moreover disabled to bring any action at law, or to prosecute any suit in equity, and among many other disabilities, they were rendered absolutely incapable of any legacy or deed of gift.

(*b*) Uniformity of public prayers, and administration of sacraments, and other rites and ceremonies was again more effectually established, and every ecclesiastical person was obliged to declare his unfeigned assent and consent to all and every thing contained and prescribed in and by the book of Common Prayer, under the penalty of perpetual disability to hold any ecclesiastical benefice or living (*c*). A declaration against transubstantiation was added to the oath of supremacy, as a necessary requisite to qualify any

(*a*) 3 Car. 1. c. 3. (*b*) 13 and 14 Car. 2. c. 4. (*c*) 25 Car. 2. c. 2.

person for an employment under government. (*a*) The ancient writ *de Heretico Comburendo* was abolished, and atheism, blasphemy, heresy, and schism were left open to the rigour of the ecclesiastical laws and censures. (*b*) A new test was framed and required of every person, against transubstantiation, the invocation of saints, and the mass, in order to exclude all Popish members from both Houses of Parliament. (*c*) The oaths of supremacy and allegiance were rather varied and exacted under fresh penalties, similar to those which had been before enacted. (*d*) All the former penalties were again confirmed and enforced against recusants, and all Papists, or reputed Papists were ordered to be moved from the cities of London and Westminster, and ten miles distant from the same. (*e*) Every Papist recusant was prohibited to have any arms, weapons, gun-powder, or ammunition in his house or elsewhere, or in the possession of any person to his use, or to have a horse in his possession of the value of five pounds, and the justices were thereby empowered to search for and seize the same; and all persons concealing the before-mentioned articles, either for themselves or others,

(*a*) 29 Car. 2. c. 9. (*b*) 30 Car. 2. St. 2. (*c*) 1 Will. and Mary, c. 8. (*d*) 1 Will. and Mary, c. 9. (*e*) 1 Will. and Mary, c. 15.

incurred

incurred the penalty of three months imprisonment, with the forfeiture of the things themselves, and treble their value. (*a*) All other Protestant dissenters from the Church of England were exempted and discharged from all the penalties imposed upon them by any of the foregoing or other penal statutes. (*b*) The presentations to all benefices belonging to Papists were vested in the two Universities. (*c*) The reward of one hundred pounds was given to every discoverer of a Romish bishop or priest; and every Romish bishop, priest, or schoolmaster of the Romish persuasion, exercising their respective functions within this realm, were adjudged to perpetual imprisonment. All persons educated in the Popish religion, not having taken the oaths within six months, after their attaining the age of 18 years, were made incapable to take, either by descent or purchase, any lands, or profits out of lands, and the next Protestant of kin was entitled to receive the rents and profits of them during the life of such recusant, without being accountable to any person whatsoever for the same, and an additional forfeiture of one hundred pounds was imposed upon all persons giving their children a Popish education, and the Chancellor was empowered to make order for the maintenance

(*a*) 1 Will. and Mary, c. 1. (*b*) 1 Will. and Mary, c. 26. (*c*) 11 and 12 Will. 3. c. 6.

of the Protestant children of Popish parents. (*a*) An oath was exacted of all persons, that no person professing the tenets of the Romish religion, could by any title whatsoever claim a right to the Crown of this realm.

(*b*) The Act of the 13th of Eliz. c. 12, for establishing the uniformity of doctrine, service, and discipline in the Church of England, was again confirmed, and security was given to the Church of Scotland. (*c*) An act was passed to prevent the growth of schism, and effectually to prevent Papists from teaching schools. (*d*) The disability of Papists presenting to ecclesiastical livings was more effectually enforced, and a power was given to the Lords Justiciary of Scotland, to put in execution all the penalties enacted by the acts of King William, against Jesuits, Priests, and other trafficking Papists in Scotland.

(*e*) All Papists were again enjoined to take the oaths and declaration, and in default thereof, within six months after their attaining the age of one-and-twenty years, or after coming from beyond seas, or into possession of land, to register their estates at their full value, under pain of forfeiting the fee simple and inheritance of the same, two thirds to the King, and the other third to the Protestant informer. (*f*)

(*a*) 13 Will. 3. c. 6. (*b*) 5 Ann. c. 5, 8. (*c*) 12 Ann. c. 7. (*d*) 12 Ann c. 14. (*e*) 1 Geo. 1. c. 55. (*f*) 3 Geo. 1, c. 18.

This forfeiture was confined to two years after the offence committed; and every conveyance of land, or interest therein, or profit thereout, made by a Papist, either by deed or will, was made void, unless inrolled within six months after such conveyance made. (*a*) The lands Papists were in the year 1723 charged with the gross sum of one hundred thousand pounds, over and above the double land tax, which they had long paid. (*b*) The oaths were again repeatedly required of all Papists, and they were again made liable to forfeit their real estates for not registering them according to the statute. (*c*) In the ensuing session further time was given to Papists to register and inroll their estates.

(*d*) The first act which passed under his late Majesty concerning Papists, was, for securing the estates of Papists conforming to the Protestant religion, against the several disabilities created by the before-mentioned Acts of Parliament, and for more effectually vesting in the two Universities the presentation of all benefices belonging to Papists; after this an act has almost annually passed for allowing further time for the inrollment of Papists' deeds, and for the relief of Protestant purchasers.

(*a*) 9 Geo. 1. c. 18. (*b*) 9 Geo. 1. c 24. (*c*) 10 Geo. 1. c. 4. (*d*) 11 Geo. 2. c. 17.

(*a*) By a late act paſſed in the eighteenth year of his preſent Majeſty, ſo much of the aforeſaid act of the 11th and 12th of King William the Third was repealed, as related to the apprehending, taking, or proſecuting of Popiſh Biſhops, Prieſts, or Jeſuits, and alſo ſo much of the ſaid act as ſubjected Popiſh Prieſts, or Jeſuits, and Papiſts or perſons profeſſing the Popiſh religion, and keeping ſchool, or taking upon themſelves the education or government, or boarding of youth within this realm, or the dominions thereto belonging, to perpetual impriſonment; and alſo ſo much of the ſaid act as diſabled perſons educated in the Popiſh religion, or profeſſing the ſame, under the circumſtances therein mentioned, to inherit, or take by deſcent, deviſe, or limitation, in poſſeſſion, reverſion, or remainder, any lands, tenements, or hereditaments, within the kingdom of England, dominion of Wales, and town of Berwick upon Tweed, and gave to the next of kin, being Proteſtant, a right to have and enjoy ſuch lands, tenements, and hereditaments; and alſo ſo much of the ſaid act as diſabled Papiſts, or perſons profeſſing the popiſh religion to purchaſe any manors, lands, profits out of lands, tenements, rents, terms, or hereditaments, within the kingdom of England, dominion of Wales, or town of Berwick upon Tweed,

(*a*) 18 Geo. 3. c. 60.

and

and made void all and singular estates, terms, and other interests or profits whatsoever out of lands to be made, suffered, or done, from and after the day therein mentioned, to or for the use or behoof of any such person or persons, or upon any trust or confidence, mediately or immediately for the relief of any such person or persons. A new form of an oath of allegiance to the reigning government was framed, and the benefit of this act was confined to those only who should take the same within six months of the passing of the act, or of their respective titles accruing.

Such is the extremity of rigour, with which the legislature of this country has, through a long series of years, punished the crime of Popery. It is foreign from my intention, to express either my approbation or disapprobation of their conduct in this point. I must however profess, that this late act of mitigation to the Papists, has, in its tendency, something singularly inconsistent, that baffles every attempt to reconcile it to common policy, and to common sense. Had the legislature, after a full investigation of the nature of Popery, declared, that it did not contain that enormity of guilt, which the punishment of it bespeaks, they must in their wisdom have withdrawn the penalties with the criminality. They now give to the professors of the Romish religion

the

the free poffeffion of their landed property, whilft by receiving the facraments according to the rites of their own church, they incur a Premunire, by which they are deprived of the King's protection, forfeit their lands, goods and chattels, and may be imprifoned for life: and whilft they exempt bifhops, priefts, and fchoolmafters, from perpetual imprifonment, they leave them liable every moment of their lives to be hanged, drawn and quartered, not only for exercifing their refpective functions, but by fetting a foot within the kingdom. A more minute attention to thefe penal ftatutes, will difclofe a wider fcene of incoherent abfurdity. On one hand, I had not the prefumption to brand the legiflature with the indelible infamy, of eftablifhing and maintaining for centuries, a tyrranical fyftem of oppreffion and injuftice: and on the other hand, even under the darkeft cloud of all my prejudices, I ever marked a wide difproportion between the feverity of the punifhment, and the malice of the crime of Popery. The proceedings of the late Parliament in favour of the Roman Catholics, ftrengthened the obfervation. I could eafily reconcile the propriety of their conduct to the general claims of humanity; whilft no one particular objection againft Popery was thereby cleared up or anfwered. Vitiated as our minds are, we fwallow in

prejudices

prejudices in the grofs, which can be only done away in the minuteft retail. I call every affection of the mind a prejudice, which difpofes it againft any opinion, or fet of men, without fully difclofing the grounds and reafons for the averfion. An implacable hatred of Popery was fyftematically infufed into my mind, in the pliancy of youth; and fuch has been the general cafe of moft men in this country. And I conceive the cafe to be as general, that in their riper years, they are as ignorant of the reafons of their prejudice, as they were when they firft imbibed it. For my own fatisfaction, I have carefully endeavoured to attain an impartial knowledge of the Romifh belief; and I fhall faithfully fubmit to the public, the knowledge which I have thus obtained, with the view of producing juftice to all parties. In the probability of human events, the total fuppreffion or toleration of Popery will foon become a fubject of Parliamentary difcuffion.

Such of the public who think at all, will have an inclination to know, what the real guilt of Popery is; the cry of which has lately raifed fuch a ferment in the nation: fuch of them as have any national concern, will find themfelves under the ftricteft obligation of learning it. Every one will readily excufe me, when I fuppofe him as little converfant with the real tenets

tenets of Popery as I was, before I made the late enquiries into the truth of them. Few men, who profess no employment, will make that a subject of their studies, which affords neither amusement or benefit: those who are engaged in any employment, whether private or public, will not readily afford themselves the leisure time for doing it. Thus from the neglect of examining into the truth, one part of the nation is most unjustly oppressed, or the legislature is most unjustly accused of tyranny.

I have frequently remarked, that in all disputes, the general ground of difference arises from the misrepresentation or misconception of the state of the case by the adverse party. In the present instance, the fact strictly verified my observation. I applied to such of my acquaintance for information, whom I thought the most capable of giving it to me; and to such of our books, from which I expected the most light upon the subject. The result of my enquiries, was a general confirmation of those early prejudices, which had prepossessed my mind from its infancy, against Popery and its professors. And to speak freely, I could deduce no other conclusion from the premises, either as an Englishman, or as a member of the Church of England, but that *Papists were criminals by profession,*

profession, and by principle enemies and traitors to their King, their country, and their God. Now that men of this description should find favour, and mercy, and indulgence from an enlightened Parliament, in an enlightened age, without one diffentient voice, was a fact which so plainly counteracted all my opinions upon the subject, that I began to suspect the ground upon which they were founded. The suspicion gained strength from reflection, and threw me upon a fresh pursuit. The very outset convinced me, that I had hitherto learnt little more of the nature of Popery, than the severity of the laws enacted against its professors.

It has never reached my knowledge, that the nature of the crime of Popery, has ever been the object of Parliamentary inquisition. Were I not tender of derogating from the omnipotency of Parliament, I might be so bold as to assert, that the civil legislature can only pronounce judgment upon the criminality of religious opinions, in as much as they interfere with, and counteract the policy and safety of the state. If Papists are in this light criminal, let them be punished with the utmost legal severity; but let their criminality be proved; conviction without evidence is unknown to a free constitution. If they are guiltless, let their innocence be proclaimed to the nation. It is not within the possibility

ity of human occurrences, that a nation should cherish those individuals, whom the most solemn laws of the land have condemned to the ignominy and punishments of felony and treason. There is in Britons an innate principle of justice: nor will they ever brook an indulgence granted to an entire body of offenders, till the guilt of the offence is wiped away. Every Papist is in the eye of the law, as it is now written, capitally criminal: and shall the nation be supposed to judge them innocent, whilst the legislature continues solemnly to adjudge them guilty? Much deference is due to the nation: even their very prejudices are not wantonly to be sported with. They are generally taught, (and it is believed) that Papists are the avowed enemies of their country, their church, their king, their constitution. Is it not then obvious that when the legislature confers a favour upon so many thousand objects of popular hatred, a contrary declaration should precede the act of grace. Amiable as is the attribute of *mercy* in the eyes of all mankind, the dispensation of it to the unworthy, must essentially incense and irritate those, who never forfeited their claim unto it. An avowed enemy ought not to be treated with partiality and friendship: nor is it in the
nature

nature of a Briton to treat a real friend with the rigour of an avowed enemy.

If any part of the following sheets should not prove to be perfectly confonant to the tenets of the Roman Catholic Faith, the gentlemen of that persuasion will, I confide, attribute my error to every other cause than a will to mislead and misrepresent. I mean fairly and candidly to state the case. I shall endeavour to steer equally clear of panegyric and invective. Whoever maturely considers the consequences of ill-grounded prejudices in an affair of this nature, must at least commend every attempt made to remove them.

I had frequently observed one of the gentlemen, whom I before mentioned, to enter the Coffee-House where I first saw him, on the morning, after the commencement of the riots. His conversation at that time appeared to me positive and informed, though altogether unaccountable. I resolved to make this a channel of enquiry, in order to learn with certainty, the real tenets of the Romish Faith, as believed and practised by the Roman Catholics themselves. I took several opportunities of making advances to him, and soon found him to be a man as easy of access, as he was liberal in thought and discourse. When propriety would permit me, I introduced the subject of religion, and always

ways remarked that his attention grew more interested whenever I started that topic. Many loose conversations passed between us upon religion, in the course of which, I perceived this gentleman insisted chiefly upon the gross misrepresentation of the Roman Catholic doctrine, which was ever made by its adversaries. This naturally introduced my petition of having the tenets of the Roman Catholic persuasion fairly and clearly stated to me. He acceded to my request with much readiness, and delivered to me, as faithfully as my memory retains it, the following account of his religion; premising, that it was not the particular opinion of a private individual, but the universal doctrine of all Roman Catholics, of all ages, and of all countries, without an iota of difference, from the foundation of Christianity to the present day. I shall not, continued he, insist upon any of those points of faith, which are not subjects of difference between us and the reformed churches; nor shall I direct your attention to any matter of religious persuasion, to which every Roman Catholic, without distinction, is not obliged to submit his unreserved faith and belief.

There are many subjects of difference and dispute among the divines of the Roman Church; but they do not concern articles of divine faith; but relate only to such matters

matters as are of pious belief among Chriftians; and concerning which, the church in her infallible capacity has never pronounced a decifive judgment. And in fact, added he, more prejudices have been entertained againft our church, from the misconception of thefe points of difference, than from any real and fubftantial objections againft the tenets of the Roman Catholic Faith. I am convinced, that I fpeak to a man of a liberal mind, who will not impute falfities to the belief of thofe who difclaim them, or attribute the fentiments of an individual to the fenfe of a collective body, which difowns them. If, on any future occafion, you fhould chufe to examine how far my narrative is confonant with the public voice of our church, I recommend, Sir, to your perufal, the Catechifm compofed by the decree of the Council of Trent, and publifhed by command of Pope Pius the Fifth. This was the laft æcumenical meeting of our church, and whatever that Council has in its aggregate capacity decided, muft certainly be the real fenfe of the church; for every Roman Catholic believes it to be an article of his faith, that the decifion of a General Council in point of doctrine, is to be admitted as an infallible decree of the *Holy Spirit*, which the Almighty hath promifed fhall teach us all truth to the end of the world.

The

The Church of England believes with the Church of Rome every article contained in the Apoſtle's Creed, and in the Creed of St. Athanaſius; and to ſay that the former allows her children more latitude in point of belief than the latter, or that Proteſtants do not hold, as firmly as Roman Catholics, that unity of faith is neceſſary for ſalvation, would draw me into conſequences, of which you are little aware, and may perhaps, Sir, affect you in a tender part.

Nothing, replied I, can offend me, but your checking the freedom of your thoughts and words; I intreat you therefore, Sir, to continue your narration with the moſt aſſured freedom; my deſire is to learn what you really profeſs and believe yourſelves; forget that I am an inquiſitive heretic; and ſuppoſe me an ignorant proſelyte to your own communion: but above all, if your religion will permit you, admit me for the hour, to the poſſibility of attaining Heaven by my own religion, though ſomewhat different from your's. For ſurely an upright man, of any religious perſuaſion whatever, will find mercy with an all-bountiful God.

I am ſenſible, replied the Roman Catholic gentleman, that this uncharitable imputation has embittered more perſons againſt our religion, than any other conſideration whatever. Yet it is uncommonly ſtrange, that this objection ſhould ever have been

been made by a member of the Church of England. Though it may seemingly invert the order of our present discourse, to give you any information concerning your own religion, yet I shall use the freedom you have given me, and shew you what the Church of England believes and teaches in this regard; but leave the explanation of the doctrine to you. I will then inform you fully what the Roman Catholic Church teaches upon the subject, and will endeavour to explain our doctrine to your entire satisfaction. I cannot, without accusing the whole body of the Clergy of the Church of England of the most wilful perjury, suppose that there is any thing contained in the Book of Common Prayer, and the Thirty-nine Articles of your Religion, which does not meet with *their sincere and unreserved belief.* (*a*) And what is the universal doctrine of the pastors of any church, must undoubtedly be acknowledged to be the doctrine of the church, which is under their guidance and direction. Upon all the most solemn festivals in the year, the Creed of St. Athanasius makes part of your Liturgy; and the minister and people join in professing that, *Whosoever will be saved, before all things it is necessary, that he hold the Catholic faith. Which faith, except every one do keep whole*

(*a*) 13 El. c. xii.

and

and undefiled, without doubt he shall perish everlastingly. And finally, *This is the Catholic faith, which except a man believe faithfully, he cannot be saved.* And in the Eighteenth Article of your religion, it is expressly said, that *They also are to be accursed that presume to say, that every man shall be saved by the law or sect which he professeth, so that he be diligent to frame his life, according to that law and the light of nature.* Such is the doctrine of the Church of England, upon this particular subject, which I leave to your own observations and thoughts.

The Roman Catholic Church teaches after St. Paul, that there is but *one God, one Faith, one Baptism*; and that heresy (which is defined to be a voluntary and obstinate error of the mind against the true faith) is a sin, which will certainly for ever exclude those, who die guilty of it, from the kingdom of Heaven. Faith we hold to be a supernatural gift infused into us by Almighty God, which man cannot by his own strength acquire. We all receive, by Christian baptism, the true faith of Jesus Christ; and we must *voluntarily* and *obstinately* reject this faith, before we can be guilty of the sin of heresy. We are by baptism true members of the church of Christ, until we freely and knowingly reject his faith, by *voluntarily* and *obstinately* adhering to false doctrines and opinions in
defiance

defiance of the light of the true faith. You see then that our judgment upon heresy is not so very severe, since we hold, that before a man can be accountable for the malice of that sin, he must *voluntarily* and *obstinately* reject a faith, which he knows to be true, and adopt another which he knows to be false. Our belief in religious mysteries to be true, must be conformable to the existence of the mysteries in which we believe, and to be so conformable, must be one and invariably the same, as the mysteries themselves are of eternal stability; hence that necessity of unity of faith, which the Roman Catholic Church ever has, and ever will teach to be requisite for salvation, and hence the severity of her judgment against heresy, which is defined, as I before observed, to be a *voluntary and obstinate error of the mind against the true faith.*

We, Sir, believe, as well as the Church of England, what St. Athanasius says of the necessity of believing the Catholic faith, in order to be saved, to be eternally true; yet, we are far from condemning to eternal perdition, every person who is called a member of any other than the Roman Catholic Church. We believe, that every man, who, after receiving Christian baptism, shall not have forfeited his baptismal innocence by any mortal offence, or having forfeited it, shall have been reconciled to the grace of Almighty God by a perfect act of contrition, let him be of whatever sect, church, or congregation, he may, yet such a man is within the pale of the true church of Christ, and rightfully entitled to the kingdom of Heaven; and to speak my own private sentiments as an individual, I strongly believe, that fewer souls perish for the sin of heresy than for most other crimes and offences. I believe, Sir, that you and most of my acquaintance, who do not profess themselves to be members of the Roman Catholic Church, are in a constant and habitual inclination, and desire of knowing and following the true faith of Jesus Christ; nor could any worldly or human motive, prejudice, or reason whatsoever, induce you to reject the true faith, if you were convinced as I am, that it was only taught and believed by the Roman Catholic Church; for it is impossible, that any person having this inclination and desire, and acting according to it, should be guilty of the sin of heresy; such is the doctrine which renders us so very hateful in the eyes of all the reformed churches. I wish to hear the positions of the Church of England on the same subject expounded more liberally; I have said thus much to convince you, Sir, that I do not really believe you to be an *Heretic*, though ignorant of the true faith. But to proceed—

The

The Roman Catholic Church teaches that Almighty God alone, as our Creator, is to be adored; that we are to believe, and hope in him, and love him with all the powers of our soul; that we are not only to render him this internal adoration in spirit and truth, but that we are to offer to him the public sacrifice of the mass, which has been instituted as a public acknowledgment of his omnipotence over us. The same church teaches us, that the worship and honour which is paid by us to the Blessed Virgin and the Saints, is merely relative, and is called *religious*, but, because it is ultimately referred to Almighty God; that from the connection which exists between the church militant upon earth, and triumphant in Heaven, which is one and the same Church of Christ, we beg the Saints in Heaven to intercede to Almighty God in our behalf, in the same manner that we apply to our brethren upon earth to offer up their oraisons to God for the same purpose; that as this latter mode of intercession has never been thought to derogate from the powerful mediation of Jesus Christ to his eternal Father in our behalf, so the Council of Trent expressly teaches us, that the former is not open to the same objection. (*a*) "The Council " expressly declares, that we pray to Al-

---

(*a*) Part 4. Tit. Quis orandus sit?

" mighty God either to grant us favours,
" or to deliver us from evils; but because the
" Saints are more agreeable to him than we
" are, we beseech them to plead our cause,
" and obtain for us such things as we stand
" in need of; hence we use two sorts of
" prayer, widely different from each other;
" for, when we address ourselves to Al-
" mighty God, we say, *have mercy upon*
" *us, hear us, &c.* but when we pray
" to the Saints we are contented to say,
" *pray for us.*" And the same Council, in
another place, expressly and decisively declares, that, " (*a*) The Saints who reign
" with Jesus Christ offer to God their
" prayers for men, and it is good and pro-
" fitable to call upon them in a suppliant
" manner, and to have recourse to their
" aid and succour, to obtain for us the
" favours of Almighty God, by Jesus Christ
" his only Son Our Lord, who alone is Our
" Saviour and Redeemer." Thus, Sir, you
see, that our praying to the Saints to petition
favours for us of Almighty God, is no more
than a solemn application to the merits of
Jesus Christ, through which alone we can
obtain them. It is a serious charge to impute
the crime of idolatry to millions of men
indiscriminately, who have avowedly practised this usage for twelve hundred years;

(*a*) Sess. 25. de Invoc.

St. Basil, St. Ambrose, St. Hierome, St. John Chrysostome, St. Augustin, and St. Gregory Nazianzen, and numberless other holy fathers, both of the Latin and Greek Church, were then all idolaters, for they speak repeatedly of their having received this practice from their predecessors, and by their warm commendation of the usage, they endeavour to perpetuate it to posterity. (*a*) St. Augustin in the fourth century expressly said, " that it was not to be believed that " the sacrifice of the Mass was offered up " to the holy martyrs; although (according " to the usage of the church) in those days " they offered up the sacrifice upon their " holy bodies to their memories," that is, upon altars, under which their sacred reliques were deposited: and the same holy father asserts in another place, " (*b*) that " when they commemorated the remem- " brance of the martyrs in the holy sacri- " fice, it was not done to pray to God for " them, as they did for other deceased " persons, but to entreat them to join in " prayer with us to Almighty God." Here, Sir, I wish you to reflect, that St. Augustin, about 1300 years ago, talks of the sacrifice of the mass, prayers to the Saints, and prayers for the dead, as the common

(*a*) 8 de Civ. c. 17. (*b*) Tract 84. in Joan Serm. 17. de verbo Apost.

usage of the church in his days; but St. Augustin had not sufficient penetration to see the idolatry of these practices, nor was he sufficiently conversant with church history to know, when, how, and by whom these idolatrous profanations were introduced into the Church of Christ, and we now better understand the sentiments of the fathers of the first ages, than those holy fathers of the fourth century, who gathered their predecessors' doctrines from their own mouths.

I did not at this time mean to interrupt my learned friend, by disputing upon the points of faith, in which we differed; but I felt that satisfaction in his discourse, that I wished him not to pass slightly from one subject to another without informing me fully of each; I therefore replied to him, that as I supposed the Roman Catholics admitted of every part of the Holy Scriptures as infallibly true, I should esteem it a favour to be informed in what manner the Roman Catholics justified this practice of their church, (ancient as it might be) by the authority of holy writ? He reminded me that his church differed from the Church of England, in holding that Scripture alone was not a sufficient rule of faith to decide all controversies on points of religion; that, however, he would speak presently more minutely to this point of difference, and in the mean while endeavour as concisely as possible

possible to give me the satisfaction I required.

As the worship or honour which we shew to the Saints and Angels in Heaven, is often expressed before their relicks, images, or pictures, I shall premise, what the Council of Trent enjoins the faithful to believe upon this subject. (*a*) "It expressly forbids us
" to believe that there is any divinity, or
" virtue in them, for which we ought to
" reverence them, to ask any favour of them,
" or to place any confidence in them ; and
" enacts, that whatever honour is paid to
" them, shall be referred to the originals
" whom they represent, so that by the
" images which we kiss, or before which
" we kneel, we adore Jesus Christ, or ho-
" nour the Saints whom they represent."

The fundamental ground of belief necessary to justify this doctrine is, that the Saints and Angels in Heaven, know what passes here upon earth, and that they are both able and willing to intercede to God in our behalf. The church has never as yet defined in what particular manner the Saints and Angels in Heaven receive their knowledge of what passes upon earth: but it is evident from several passages of Scripture, that they really have this knowledge. What, for instance, can be more secret and hidden, than the affection of the heart, by which

(*a*) *Concil. Terid. Sess.* 25. *de Invoc.*

a sinner

a sinner returns to the grace of Almighty God? Yet it is said (Luke xv. 10.) *There is joy in the presence of the Angels of God, over one sinner that repenteth.* How shall they rejoice at what they know not? In the conversation, between Abraham and the Dives, the same Evangelist (Luke xvi. 29.) puts in the mouth of Abraham these words, *They have Moses and the Prophets, let them hear them.* Does not this suppose Abraham to have a knowledge of what passed upon earth after his death: as Moses and the Prophets did not exist, till many years after Abraham had departed out of this life. Several years also after the departure of Elijah the Prophet out of this life, it appears from the sacred text (2 Chron. xxi. 12) that he knew what passed upon earth, and testified his great care and concern to help God's people his brethren: *There came a writing to Jehoram from Elijah the Prophet, saying, thus saith the Lord God of David thy father, because thou hast not walked in the ways of Jehoshaphat thy father, &c.* Although the Church of England holds the book of Tobias to be one of the Apochrypha, yet it recommends it to be read (*a*) *for example of life, and instruction of manners:* consequently it cannot be supposed to establish or promote any idolatrous practices: and yet there we read, (Tob. xii, 15,) *Ra-*

(*a*) 6 Art. of Rel.

phael

phael one of the seven, which assist before the Lord, said unto Tobias, when thou didst pray with tears, and didst bury the dead by night, I offered thy prayer to the Lord. You must, Sir, at least allow, that the writer of the book of Tobias, whether inspired by the Holy Ghost or not, believed, as the Roman Catholic Church now does, that the angels know what passes here upon earth, that they are attentive to our good actions, and that they offer up our prayers to the Lord. We, Sir, find both *example of life and instruction of manners* in this very passage: besides, we hold after Saint Cyprian, Saint Ambrose, Saint Augustin, Saint Hierom, Saint Gregory, and the third Council of Carthage, that the book of Tobias is a part of the canonical Scripture. And every person must indiscriminately acknowledge, that this doctrine of the intercession of angels in our behalf, is no novel institution of the Romish Church, but that it is, at least, coeval with the book of Tobias. Saint Augustin quoted these words of Saint (1 Paul Cor. xiii. 9. 10) " *For we know in part, and prophecy in part; but when that, which is perfect is come, then that which is in part shall be done away,*" to prove that the Saints and Angels in Heaven have a more perfect knowledge of what passes here upon earth than we have, who live in it.

It is evident from many texts of the Old
and

and New Testament, that the Saints and Angels of God, are both able and willing to help us, by their prayers and intercession. (Gen. xlviii. 16) Jacob acknowledges himself to have been delivered from evils by the help of an angel. *The angel, which redeemed me from all evil, &c.* So Job's friends following the belief and practice of their time, spoke thus to him: *Call now if there be any that will answer thee, and to which of the Saints wilt thou turn?* (Job. v. 1.) The Septuagint here interpret the word *Saints* to mean *Angels*. There cannot be framed a more formal intercession to the Almighty in behalf of Judah, than the prayer of the Angel, as it is expressed (Zechar. i. 12.) *Then the Angel of the Lord answered and said, O Lord of Hosts, how long wilt thou not have mercy on Jerusalem, and on the cities of Judah, against which thou hast had indignation these three-score and ten years?* And what was the effect of the Angel's prayer. *And the Lord answered the Angel, good words, comfortable words.* Now, Sir, as you believe the book of Zechariah to be infallible Scripture, do you still seriously believe that these afflicted Jews would have been guilty of idolatry, by beseeching this Angel (who was both willing and able to obtain redress for them) to intercede to Almighty God in their behalf. The Lord would certainly never have encouraged an idolatrous

idolatrous practice in the Jews, by *good words, comfortable words.*

In the New Testament, although perhaps you will say, that the sense of the Book of Revelations, is still to be revealed, yet no person will pretend to accuse Saint John of describing any idolatrous practice or usage carried on before the Throne of Almighty God. Yet (Rev. viii. 3.) we read, that *another angel came and stood at the altar having a golden censer; and there was given unto him much incense, that he should offer it, with the prayers of all Saints upon the golden altar, which was before the throne. And the smoke of the incense, which came with the prayers of the saints, ascended up before God, out of the Angel's hand.* Behold here the Angel performing the office of presenting our prayers to Almighty God. What idolatry therefore can there be, in desiring these Angels to fulfil the charge imposed upon them by Almighty God?

As to the external honour of worship, which we pay to the Saints and blessed spirits in Heaven, we find it warranted in numberless instances in Holy Writ. (Joshua v. 14. 15.) At the appearance of the Angel, *Joshua fell on his face to the earth, and did worship, and said unto him, what saith my Lord unto his servant? And the captain of the Lord's host said unto Joshua: loose thy shoe from off thy foot: for the place whereon thou standest is holy. And Joshua did so.* And in another part of the Revelations, these words are spoken to the Angel of Philadelphia, (Rev. iii. 9.) *Behold I will make them come and worship before thy feet.* External motions are but figurative or expressive of the internal affections of the heart: to bend the knee or head to an earthly prince, or to bow to each other, might with as much reason be called idolatry: as this relative honour, which we pay to the chosen and glorified servants of Almighty God. Would it not, Sir, either raise your indignation, or your pity, if a Quaker were to accuse every member of the Church of England of idolatry, because they are observed to kneel before the sacrament of the Lord's Supper, which they hold to be only a sign or figure of Christ's body: or because they are frequently seen kneeling and praying in their churches before their altar-pieces, which are representations of Christ and his Saints: for, it is immaterial, whether such representations be in alto or basso relievo, upon canvas or in full projection. Again, we read in Saint Paul (1. Cor. xi. 27.) *Whoever shall eat this bread or drink this cup of the Lord unworthily, shall be guilty of the body and blood of our Lord.* And (v. 29) *For he that eateth and drinketh unworthily, eateth and drinketh damnation to himself.* Now Sir, in your

principles

principles, the sacrament, is but *a sign or figure* of Christ's body, and yet an abuse of this *sign or figure*, is punished with eternal damnation, as an abuse of the body itself. If *relative abuse* then meet with such rigorous punishment, can you suppose that *relative honour and respect* paid to the same *sign or figure* shall not be rewarded. One more word before I leave this subject: sound conveys through the ears, as light does through the eyes, different representations to the mind: the vibration of the air acting upon the organs of our hearing, and the reflection of light acting upon the organs of our sight, may raise the same idea, affection, or representation in the mind: we may be strucken with the same reverential awe, when we behold the sacred name of Jesus, printed or engraved, as when we hear it pronounced: and if it be idolatry to bend the knee in one instance, it is equally so in the other. Yet Saint Paul saith expressly, (Phil. ii. 10.) *that at the name of Jesus every knee should bow.* In short, if there could be no other use of images, but such as is idolatrous, do you suppose that Almighty God, would have ordered the Jews (prone as they ever were to idolatry) to adorn the Ark and the temple with the figures or statues of cherubims?

The

The honour which we shew to the relics of saints, and to the very places where they are kept, or where the Saints themselves have lived, or performed any particular act of virtue, or miracle, naturally flows from the foregoing doctrines, and I will shortly shew you upon what scriptural authority we ground this doctrine. We see in the old law that such respect and honour was due to the Ark, which was only a portable chapel, (Heb. ix. 4) *Wherein was the golden pot that had manna, and Aaron's rod that budded, and the tables of the covenant*, that because the men of Bethshemesh had irreverently looked into the Ark of the Lord, (1 Sam vi. 19.) *he smote of thy people fifty thousand threescore and ten men.* Honour and reverence then to these sacred relics was not idolatry at that time. The cloak of Elijah had, I suppose, no intrinsic virtue in it more than the cloak of any other Jew of his time, and was probably made of the same materials and in the same form with others. (2 Kings, ii. 14.) yet Elijah, in order to work the miracle of dividing the waters, *took the mantle of Elijah that fell from him, and smote the waters, and said, Where is the Lord God of Elijah? and when he had also smitten the waters, they parted hither and thither; and Elijah went over.* It would be now accounted the most superstitious and idolatrous bigotry to suppose, that a dead man could be revived by the touch of a

Saint's

Saint's relics; yet Almighty God did not surely encourage or countenance idolatry or superstition, by working this very miracle? (2 Kings, xiii. 21.) *for when the dead man was let down, and touched the bones of Elijah, he revived and stood upon his feet.* The open common field of Jericho was no more holy than any other part of the country, yet the angel told Joshua, *(ubi supra)* to loose the shoes of his feet, for that the place whereon he stood was holy; and why? because sanctified by the miraculous apparition of an Angel. There is the most particular mention made in the New Testament of the first Christians applying relics to the ends of curing diseases, casting out Devils, &c. (Acts, xix. 11. 12.) *And God wrought special miracles by the hands of Paul. So that from his body were brought unto the sick, handkerchiefs or aprons, and the diseases departed from them, and the evil spirits went out of them.* I could cite many more passages which warrant this doctrine and practice, but will proceed to other points of difference between us.

The grand and essential difference between the Roman Catholic and every other reformed church, is the attribute of infallibility of doctrine, which our church assumes to itself; this is the leading principle of the Roman Catholic faith, it is the corner stone upon which every individual builds his faith, and

and the folution of all his doubts and difficulties concerning it; he who believes a church to be infallible, muft of neceffity fubmit to all her decifions, and her attribute of infallibility alone can make her a competent judge in all matters of controverfy. Divine faith is effentially of a different complexion from human belief: by the former we fubject our underftanding to the moft incomprehenfible myfteries, and firmly believe what we neither fee or underftand; by the latter we can only affent to fuch things as fall under the teftimony of our fenfes, or within the comprehenfion of our intellectual faculties. Both you, Sir, and I agree in the neceffity of believing in the myfteries of the Trinity and Incarnation, but neither your reafon or mine can by the force of nature comprehend either of thefe myfteries; in fact, if we could, they would from that inftant ceafe to be myfteries; but if I am in any one inftance obliged to believe what I do not, and cannot poffibly comprehend, it would be rafhnefs to feek any rule of faith which was liable to error and deceit; we Roman Catholics, therefore, univerfally hold this fundamental maxim, that the firft effential quality of the true Church of Chrift is, *infallibility of doctrine*; for Jefus Chrift who neither can deceive, or be deceived, hath promifed, (Mat. xxviii. 20.) *Lo, I am with you always, even unto the end of the world.*
And

And again, (Mat. xvi. 19.) *Thou art Peter, and upon this rock will I build my church, and the gates of hell shall not prevail against it;* and further, (John xiv. 16.) *He shall give you another comforter, that he may abide with you for ever, the spirit of truth, for he dwelleth with you, and shall be in you.* Now the Apostles, not being to exist for ever, and these promises being to last for ever, at least to the end of the world, we must conclude that they were made as well to the successors of the Apostles, as to the apostles themselves.

If then truth and infallibility are distinctive marks of the true Church of Christ, my reason for adhering to the Roman Catholic Church is conclusive to demonstration; every other church upon earth teaches herself to be fallible; and if any of such churches be the Church of Christ, her doctrine must be true, and it must be also true that she is fallible, but if false, then is her infallibility out of the question; as therefore no church which teaches herself to be fallible, can possibly be infallible in her doctrine, so that church alone which teaches herself to be infallible, can even claim the attribute of infallibility. If the Church of Christ were fallible in her doctrine, he never could have so rigorously enjoined us to obey it. (Mat. xviii. 17.) *And if he shall neglect to hear them, tell it unto the churc , but if he neglect to hear the church,*

let

let him be unto thee as an heathen man and a publican. Verily I say unto you, whatsoever ye shall bind on earth, shall be bound in Heaven; and whatsoever ye shall loose on earth, shall be loosed in Heaven. Upon the strength of this and many similar passages, the doctrine and practice of the Roman Catholic Church is founded. If any difference or dispute arise among the faithful, concerning any article of divine faith, she has immediate recourse to a general council, and such decisions she holds to be the infallible dictates of the spirit of truth; it is worthy our attention to remark how minutely this practice of our church is warranted by the holy Scripture; we find (Acts xv.) that *no small dissention and disputation* had been among the faithful concerning the necessity of Circumcision, therefore *they determined that Paul and Barnabas, and certain other of them should go up to Jerusalem unto the Apostles and others about this question, and the apostles and elders came together to consider of this matter;* there you see not only the Apostles themselves, but their successors making part of that Church which was guided by the infallible truth of the Holy Ghost, and although the Holy Ghost particularly assisted at it, yet we read *that there was much disputing in it,* and in the end they come to this formal decision: *It seemeth good unto the Holy Ghost, and unto us, &c.* Hence have

have our general councils ever followed the example of this first meeting of the church, by declaring also, that their decisions are according to the direction and guidance of the Holy Ghost, which God hath promised *shall guide us into all truth.* (John, xvi. 12.)

Thus the Roman Catholic Church following the spirit of the Apostles, and the literal and obvious sense of the holy Scripture, believes the Church of Christ to be ever guided by the Holy Ghost in all truth, and consequently allows her to be the supreme judge of all controversies, and the interpreter of the word of God, and upon the strength of this doctrine does every individual in our church satisfy and arm his mind and conscience, under all doubts and perplexities, by the mere knowledge he has of what his church teaches. It would certainly be unjust if Almighty God should oblige us to captivate our understandings to a faith, which (being fallible) might lead us into error, deceit, and falsehood: but it is certain that Almighty God does require of us this captive submission of our reason to faith; (2 Cor. x. 4, 5, 6.) *For the weapons of our warfare are not carnal, but mighty through God, to the pulling down of strong holds, casting down imaginations, and every high thing that exalteth itself against the knowledge of God, and bringing into captivity every thought to the obedience of Christ, and having in readiness to revenge*

revenge all disobedience when your obedience is fulfilled Now, in order more effectually to render this submission or obedience practical, Almighty God hath established an ecclesiastical hierarchy in his church, that its members may never be left in ignorance for want of instruction, or in darkness for want of a visible head upon earth. (Ephes. iv. 11.) *And he gave some apostles, and some prophets, and some evangelists, and some pastors and teachers for the perfecting of the saints, for the work of the ministry, for the edifying of the body of Christ, till we all come in the unity of faith, and of the knowledge of the Son of God unto a perfect man, unto the measure of stature of the fulness of Christ; that we may from henceforth be no more children tossed to and fro, and carried about with every wind of doctrine, by the slight of men, and cunning craftiness, whereby they lie in wait to deceive, but speaking the truth in love, may grow up into him in all things, which is the head, even Christ.*

Seeing then that Jesus Christ would have his church to be one, and solidly built upon this unity, he established and instituted the spiritual supremacy of St. Peter, to maintain and cement it. Therefore the Roman Catholics acknowledge this same spiritual supremacy to exist in the successors of St. Peter; for if it were necessary in the infant church, even living the apostles, in order to keep the faithful *in the unity of faith,* and preserve

serve them *from being tossed to and fro, and carried about with every wind of doctrine by the flight of men, and cunning craftiness,* how much more necessary was it in after ages, when the evils, which, according to St. Paul, it was established to prevent, were multiplied and magnified. We do not believe that Jesus Christ gave any other than a spiritual or ecclesiastical power, pre-eminence or authority to St. Peter, when he said (Mat. xvi 19,) *And I will give unto thee the keys of the kingdom of Heaven,* nor do we allow any other to his successors: but as the power itself is merely *spiritual,* so is the title unto it merely of a *spiritual nature.* A man can only become a successor of the apostles by ordination, and such alone can partake of a share in the ecclesiastical hierarchy; no degree therefore whatever of spiritual power or jurisdiction can possibly be acquired by temporal means. *My kingdom is not of this world.* We are therefore bound strictly by our consciences, not to acknowledge any spiritual power, pre-eminence, or authority, in any temporal royalty or other magistracy whatever. If we believe that Jesus Christ *gives unto any man the keys of the kingdom of Heaven,* we cannot believe that it is in the power of any man, or any body of men, to impede and prevent, to transmit and transpose, to extinguish and annull, this gift of Jesus Christ, at his and their will and pleasure.

These

These are incidents of *temporal* power, not of *spiritual* jurisdiction. We refuse therefore the oath when tendered to us, of spiritual supremacy, whether it go to acknowledge it in a man, in a woman, or in an infant. As the submission or obedience which the primitive Christians paid to the spiritual supremacy of St. Peter did not in any degree interfere with their civil allegiance to their respective powers, so the acknowledgment of the Pope's supremacy, has no other effect upon a Roman Catholic subject of this country, than to enforce his acquiescence in its laws and constitution; the very power to which he pays his spiritual submission, obliges him, under the pain of eternal reprobation, to believe, that he owes submission and obedience to the temporal powers which the law places over him, according to the frequent injunctions to that effect imposed upon us by the holy Scriptures, where we are also particularly warned not to withold our obedience and submission on account of the personal vices or errors of those, whom the law invests with the civil powers; we are equally commanded to obey the most wicked and idolatrous Princes, as the Jews were commanded to obey the Scribes and Pharisees, who had sitten upon the chair of Moses; and we hold ourselves equally obliged *not to do according to their works*; the line is easily drawn between that which

which belongs to Cæsar, and that which belongs to God,

Tradition is another essential difference between the Roman Catholic and all other reformed churches. Jesus Christ having founded his church upon *preaching, tradition* consequently was the first rule of Christian faith: and afterwards, when the Scriptures of the New Testament were joined to that rule, the word of God so preached, lost nothing of its authority: we therefore receive with equal veneration, whatever was taught by the Apostles, whether in writing or by word of mouth, according to that of St. Paul (2. Thess. ii. 15.) *Therefore brethren, stand fast and hold the traditions, which ye have been taught, whether by word or by our epistle.*

If the written word alone were necessary for salvation, then no person could have been saved without it. If so, what was the fate of all those souls, who lived before the books of Moses were written; which time included the space of two thousand and four hundred years, according to the best chronologists. What was the fate of all those Christians who departed out of this life before the New Testament was written: for Saint John did not write his gospel till the ninety-ninth year after the birth of Christ. Again, one part of the written law, is of equal authority with another,

ther, consequently Almighty God could never have deprived his Church, of any part of the written law; yet it is evident that many parts of the Scripture have been intirely lost. A learned Divine of Germany has proved, that not fewer than twenty books of the prophetical penmen of the Holy Ghost, have totally perished. But not to go upon equivocal proofs, some few texts of the Canonical books of Scripture which still exist, will demonstrate my assertion. (Job. x. 13) *Is not this written in the Book of Jasher?* (1. Kings iv. 32.) *Solomon spake three thousand proverbs, and his songs were a thousand and five.* 1.) Chron. xxix. 29.) *Now the the acts of David the King, first and last, behold they are written in the Book of Samuel the Seer, and in the Book of Nathan the Prophet, and in the Book of Gad the Seer.* (2. Chron ix. 29.) *Now the rest of the acts of Solomon, first and last, are they not written in the Books of Nathan the Prophet, and in the prophecy of Ahijah the Shilonite, and in the visions of Iddo the Seer?* None of these last mentioned books now exist: and yet it is palpable that they contained the written word of God, according to that of Saint Peter. (2 Ep. Pet. 1. 20) *Knowing this first, that no prophecy of the Scripture is of private interpretation. But the prophecy came not in old time by the will of man, but holy men of God spake, as they were moved*

moved by the Holy Ghost. Does it not follow, that we have not now the whole word of God, as it was written? Now if the written word were our *sole* rule of Faith, it would not have been handed down to us in this curtailed state. A Roman Catholic is under no difficulty of selecting the true apostolic traditions, from the legendary tales and anecdotes, which ignorance or malice have endeavoured to confound and blend together. He submits his faith to such traditions only, which the church has admitted and declared to be really apostolical. Although in theory, you reject this doctrine, yet in practice you admit it in many instances. For upon what clear text of Scripture does the Church of England reject some part of the Scriptures as Apocrypha, and admit others as canonical, which are quoted in no other part of Scriptures? Upon what text of Scripture does she ground the change of the Jewish Sabbath into the Sunday?

Before I speak of the sacraments of the Roman Catholic Church, I shall endeavour to prevent an objection which is often raised against the external forms and ceremonies of the Romish Church. These, Sir, are merely instituted to attract the attention of the parties assisting, and to remind them of the mysteries they are intended to represent. The Roman Catholic Church is moreover

moreover so extremely tenacious of her distinctive characteristic of *unity of faith*, that she will, as nearly as possible, have the faithful even adhere to an apparent uniformity of service. Yet as these ceremonies and forms make no part of the Christian faith, so in different countries they frequently differ. The philosopher may very plausibly at first condemn every appearance of mummery, form and foppery; but the Christian will not hastily set up his own judgment in defiance of the wisdom of the Gospel. Whether Almighty God was adored under the law of nature, of Moses, or of Jesus Christ, the external act of religion was the same, as to substance and effect. In the law of nature we know of no particular ordinances of any form or ceremony whatever. And we see Jacob, (Gen. xxviii. 18.) *Arising in the morning, took the stone that he had laid under his head, and erected it for a title or monument, and poured out oil upon the top of it.* Now to argue philosophically hereupon, we shall find in this waste of oil upon the dry stone, nothing either tending to the service or glory of Almighty God: and a philosophic eye witness of the fact, would undoubtedly have turned it into contempt, ridicule, and raillery. But Almighty God approved of the fact, appearing to Jacob, and saying (Gen. xxxi. 13.) *I am the God of Bathel*

Bathel, where thou didst anoint the stone, and didst vow thy vow to me. We all know that the law of Moses consisted of types and figures, of the future mysteries of the Christian Religion: and that the Jewish ordinances ceased upon the establishment of Christianity. But let us convey in idea one of these philosophical reasoners into the Temple of Jerusalem: let him there behold the statues of the cherubims, and the other decorations of the temple, let him examine minutely the mysteries and symbolical trappings of the officiating pontiff, let him attend to the very singular actions, gestures, and movements of the priests and Levites, such as (Exod. xxix. 20.) the anointing of the right ears and the thumbs, and great toes of their priests with ram's blood, and other forms and ceremonies as apparently mimical and absurd. What judgment would he frame upon such strange appearances? Could he, without a very peculiar gift of faith, believe them to be the absolute and express orders and commands of the omnipotent Creator and ruler of the universe? We, Sir, know them to have been such, and consequently believe that there is no action so trivial, by which Almighty God may not be glorified.

In the Christian legislation, we find no set form of ceremonies, which Jesus Christ hath ordered to be used. But if we believe, that

that he became incarnate, not only for our redemption, but alſo to ſet us an example for our imitation, we ſhall find that he ſeldom or ever performed any extraordinary action by virtue of his divinity, which was not accompanied with ſome external form to attract the attention of the beholders. So in the cure of the deaf and dumb man (Mark. vii 32.) *Firſt*, He took him from the multitude apart. *Secondly*, He put his finger into his ears. *Thirdly*, Spitting, he touched his tongue. *Fourthly*, He looked up to Heaven. *Fifthly*, He groaned. *Sixthly*, He uſed a word which required a ſpecial explanation, ſaying, *Epheta*, that is, be opened. And ſo moſt of the miracles which he performed were attended with ſome ſuch external forms and ceremonies. So at the inſtitution of the bleſſed ſacrament of the Euchariſt, (Mark xiv. 14.) he made choice of *a large upper room, furniſhed and prepared*, as more ſuitable to the ſolemnity of the occaſion: then *he firſt waſhed his diſciples feet*, to teach us to prepare ourſelves for this divine ſacrament by acts of humility and charity: then *ſitting down, he took bread, gave thanks, bleſſed it, brake it*, &c. Where then is the ſuperſtition, in our prieſts uſing the like ceremonies at the conſecration of the elements of bread and wine, in the ſacrifice of the Holy Maſs? Or in their adorning their churches and chapels upon
ſolemn

solemn festivals? But to proceed to the sacraments.

The Roman Catholic Church holds seven distinct sacraments, because she finds seven such holy signs or ceremonies, to the due application of which the gift of inward grace is annexed.

Thus (John iii. 5.) *Except a man be born of water, he cannot enter into the kingdom of God.* Behold here, water the outward sign, and the right to the kingdom of Heaven, the grace annexed. And this is the sacrament of baptism.

(Acts viii. 14.) *Now when the Apostles, which were at Jerusalem, heard that Samaria had received the word of God, they sent unto them Peter and John: who, when they were come down, prayed for them that they might receive the Holy Ghost. For as yet he was fallen upon none of them: only they were baptized in the name of the Lord Jesus. Then laid they their hands on them, and they received the Holy Ghost.* The imposition of hands is the outward sign of confirmation, the receipt of the Holy Ghost is the grace annexed thereto. The Roman Catholic Church has immemorially used the Holy Chrism, or blessed oil in the administration of this sacrament, to denote the peculiar unction of the Holy Ghost, which is conferred by it.

The outward signs of the Sacrament of Penance, are the dispositions of the penitent, and absolution of the Priest, by virtue of the power given him by Jesus Christ. (John, xx. 22.) *And when he had said this he breathed on them, and said unto them, receive ye the Holy Ghost. Whose soever sins ye remit, they are remitted unto them; and whose soever sins ye retain, they are retained.* The grace annexed is the forgiveness of sin. *But Thomas, one of the twelve, called Didymus, was not with them when Jesus came;* yet no man denies that this power was also given to Thomas: and the Church of England holds this power given to her ministers as fully as we do, and uses the identical prayer or form of absolution, which the Roman Catholic Church also does. *(Vide the Book of Common Prayer in the Visitation of the Sick.) Our Lord Jesus Christ, who hath left power to his Church to absolve all sinners, who truly repent and believe in him, of his great mercy forgive thee thine offences, and by his authority committed to me, I absolve thee from all thy sins, in the name of the Father, and of the Son, and of the Holy Ghost. Amen.*

(Jam. v. 14.) *Is any sick among you? let him call for the elders of the church, and let them pray over him, anointing him with oil in the name of the Lord; and the prayer of faith shall save the sick, and Lord shall raise*

raise him up, and if he have committed sins, they shall be forgiven him. Behold here a visible outward sign, to which grace is plainly annexed, and this is our sacrament of *extreme unction*, which the Church of England totally rejects, not only as a sacrament, but even as a pious usage, although she admits of the Epistle of St. James to be canonical Scripture.

The sacrament of holy orders is as clearly warranted by Scripture as any other seven sacraments of our church, (1 Tim. iv. 14.) *Neglect not the gift that is in thee, which was given thee by prophecy, by laying on of the hands of the presbytery.* (2 Tim. i. 6.) *Wherefore I put thee in remembrance that thou stir up the gift of God, which is in thee, by the putting on of my hands.* Is not the imposition of hands an external sign? Is not the gift of God, grace annexed thereto?

As to matrimony, the Roman Catholic church believes, that although both before and under the law of Moses, it was a holy institution, yet that it was no sacrament, but that Jesus Christ raised it to that dignity in the law of grace. The matter of the sacrament, or the outward sign thereof; has always been the same, viz, the mutual consent of the parties contracting, made to each other by words or signs for the present, and not for any future time, (for the Priest assists as a witness, not as the minister of the

the sacrament.) Our Lord, speaking of the marriage of Adam and Eve, and of the usage thereof among Jews, (Mat. xix. 5.) Mat. x. 9.) did then abrogate the law of Moses, which in many instances permitted husband and wife to be separated. *What therefore God hath joined together, let no man put asunder*, of which passage St. Paul speaks in his letter to the (Ephesians, v. 31) *For this cause shall a man leave his father and mother, and shall be joined unto his wife, and they two shall be one flesh; this is a great mystery, but I speak in Christ and the church.* Το μυστεριον τουτο μεγα εςιν; εγω δε λεγω εις Χριςον και εις την εκκλησιαν. (Thess. iv. 4.) *That every one of you should know to possess his vessel in sanctification and honour, not in the lust of concupiscence, even as the Gentiles who know not God;* these are the effects of the grace annexed to the holy sacrament of matrimony, of which sanctifying grace he gives further proof, (Ephes. v. 23.) *For the husband is the head of the wife, even as Christ is the head of the Church.*

The doctrine of the Roman Catholic Church concerning the Blessed Sacrament of the Eucharist, contains that essential difference between the Church of England and the Church of Rome, to which every British subject is bound to subscribe upon oath, before he can partake of the common rights of nature and society in his native country.

try. The doctrine of *Transubstantiation* depends upon the interpretation which the Roman Catholic Church gives to those words of the holy Scripture, which relates to this blessed sacrament of the altar. We are by our faith obliged to understand the Scriptures in that sense, which the Church declares in her infallible capacity they contain; but if the word of God were of private interpretation, is it not obvious that it is as great a stretch of power, to force upon a whole nation the Belief, that by the words, *this is my body*, Jesus Christ meant to assure us that it *was not his body*, as it is, to explain them in their obvious and literal meaning? Permit me to suppose that a native of some idolatrous nation, had through the strength of his own reasoning, resolved to abandon his idolatry, and embrace the Christian faith; that he had in his passage to England diligently read over the Scripture; that he had not even heard of any differences between the professors of the Christian faith; that upon his landing he had accidentally applied successively to a Roman Catholic and a Protestant, to clear up some doubts which had arisen in his mind, concerning this very passage of the Scripture. He expresses his wonder at the Goodness of Almighty God in giving us his body in this mysterious manner, but acknowledges the mystery to be beyond his comprehension.

He is informed by the Roman Catholic, that *no prophecy of the Scripture is of private interpretation*, (2 Ep. Pet. i. 20.) that the Church of Christ is the infallible interpreter of the holy Scripture; that this myftery is the moft incomprehenfible of all the myfteries of our religion to human underftanding, but that the meafure of our intellectual abilities, is not the ground of our faith; that we are to fubmit to this as we do to other myfteries, which are equally above our comprehenfion; for that it is as naturally impoffible that one fhould be three, and that three fhould be one, that God fhould become man, that he fhould die and rife again, as it is, that a body fhould exift without extenfion, and that accidents fhould remain without their fubftance, as is the cafe of the real body of Chrift in the Eucharift.

He is informed by the Proteftant, that the word of God, which is delivered to us in the Scripture, is to be underftood and interpreted by the private fenfe and judgment of every individual; that it is idolatry and fuperftition to underftand any thing more by thefe words, than that the bread after confecration is not the body of Chrift; and that as a proof of the truth which he advanced, the legiflature had exacted, under the moft fevere and capital punifhments, an oath from every fubject of this country, that

that he believes by the words of Christ, *The bread which I will give is my flesh,* (John, vi. 51.) *for my flesh is meat indeed, and my blood is drink indeed;* that the *bread which he will give is not his flesh,* and *that his flesh is not meat indeed, and that his blood is not drink indeed.*

The Neophite being amazed at this jarring difference between two persons, whom he supposed to profess the same religion, immediately resolved to pursue no longer a faith, which upon the first blush disclosed such palpable contradiction. He felt *himself* totally inadequate to the interpretation of the Scriptures, in reading which, he had notwithstanding experienced much consolation and satisfaction. He found it was necessary that there should somewhere exist, an unerring interpreter of the word of God; for to apply to those who pretend to be guided by nothing more certain than their own sense and judgment, was to propose doubt to doubt, and to remove difficulties by insuring uncertainty; that he could by no means, upon the strength of his own judgment, even suppose, much less swear, that the words, *this is my flesh,* mean the very reverse, *this is not my flesh.* He could not moreover reconcile to his own ideas, the interference of the civil legislature with the interpretation of the word of God; in a word, he determined to stay no longer in a country, where the religion profeſſed to leave the ſenſe of the word of God to the free interpretation of individuals, whilſt the legiſlature in ſupport of that ſame religion, obliged every ſubject, univerſally, by oath, and under capital puniſhments, to one alternative. His judgment was too ſolid to entertain even a thought of returning to his ancient idolatry; he ſet off in purſuit of a religion, which would afford more certainty and leſs contradiction, and of a country, where, if he were free to chooſe his own faith, his election might not deprive him of his fortune or his life.

I have only to add, that it would be inſolence and preſumption to attempt to account for this or any other myſtery, by natural or human means.

The principal objections againſt the Maſs are grounded upon the denial of the real preſence; having ſaid ſo much of that, I ſhall barely expound the doctrine of the Roman Catholic Church concerning the Maſs; when Jeſus Chriſt, at his laſt ſupper, ſaid, (Luke xxii. 19.) *Do this in remembrance of me*, the Roman Catholic Church teaches, that he did then offer up his body and blood in ſacrifice, in an unbloody manner; what Jeſus Chriſt then gave for us for remiſſion of ſins, was his body and blood, preſent in the conſecrated bread, (which was afterwards to ſuffer in a bloody manner upon Mount Calvary,)

Calvary,) and this was properly a propitiatory offering, such as is offered up daily by the Priests of our Church. The words of the (Acts, xiii. 2.) *As they were ministering to the Lord, and fasting,* λειτουργουντων δε αυτων τω Κυριω και νηςευωντων, have been through all antiquity understood of the sacrifice of the Mass. Observe also, that the Scripture particularly mentions that they did it *fasting*, and such is the universal usage of our Church to this day.

The administration of the Sacrament to the laity under one kind, is only a point of discipline in the Roman Catholic Church, and was introduced into general usage to prevent abuses, by spilling the consecrated wine, &c. but the Church is warranted in the usage by the express authority of the Holy Scriptures; for where the body of Christ is, there also is the blood of Christ, and whosoever receives under one kind, receives the full effect of this Divine Sacrament, according to that of (St. John, vi. 48.) *I am the bread of life. Your fathers did eat manna in the wilderness, and are dead. This is the bread which cometh down from Heaven, that a man may eat thereof, and not die. I am the living bread which came down from Heaven, if any man eat of this bread, he shall live for ever, and the bread which I will give is my flesh, which I will give for the life of the world.* (1 Cor. xi. 27.) *Wherefore whoso-*

ever shall eat this bread, or drink this cup of the Lord unworthily, shall be guilty of the body and blood of the Lord. Ὥστε ὃς ἂν ἐσθίῃ τον ἀρτον τȣτον ἢ πίνῃ το ποτέριον του Κυρίου ἀναξίως, ἔνοχος ἔσται του σώματος και αἵματος του Κυρίου. Here you see that whosoever receives under *either* kind disjunctively, in an unworthy state, is made guilty both of the body and the blood of our Lord conjunctively. (Luke, xxiv. 30.) *And it came to pass as he sat at meat with them, he broke bread, and blessed it, and broke and gave it to them: and their eyes were opened, and they knew him.* Here our Blessed Saviour himself gave the Communion under one kind, and we behold the effects of the Grace of the Sacrament, by their knowing him to be their Saviour.

There are several other usages or points of discipline in our Church, which are as much condemned by the reformed Churches as the articles of faith, by which we differ from each other, such are praying in an unknown tongue and the celibacy of Priests. The Roman Catholic Church ordains it as a point of discipline, that the public service of the church shall be said in the Latin tongue; for it is certain, that the uniformity of a dead language is best calculated to preserve the uniformity of the service; yet, to shew that it is but an ecclesiastical ordinance, the Church frequently dispenses with it, and permits the mass to be said in

the

the Greek language; this public prayer in a dead language will not appear ftrange to thofe, who confider, that *from the tranfmigration of Babylon unto Chrift, fourteen generations*, the public fervice in the Jewifh fynagogue was performed in a language unknown to the vulgar Jews; for the Syriac language which the Jews then fpoke, was as different from the old Hebrew, in which the Scriptures were written, as the Greek tongue is different from the Latin; yet was the ufage carried on under the eyes of our Bleffed Lord, and never was difapproved of by him. So, when he cried out from the crofs, *Eli, Eli, Lamafabacthani*, the Jews underftood not what he faid, and St. Matthew, who wrote his Gofpel in the Syriac language, interprets the words into the Syriac, that they may be underftood by thofe who read his Gofpel.

Every thinking man knows but too well the inconveniences which daily fpring from the marriages of Clergymen; but to pafs over the temporal difadvantages which arife to the Church therefrom, I fhall fhew you what St. Paul fays to this fubject, (1 Cor. vii. 32.) *He that is unmarried careth for the things that belong to the Lord, how he may pleafe the Lord; but he that is married careth for the things that are of this world, how he may pleafe his wife.* Every Prieft muft have attained the age of twenty-four years before he he can be ordained; he must consequently not be ignorant of what he undertakes, when at receiving holy orders, he promises to lead a single life, and vows his chastity to Almighty God. And (Numb. xxx. 11.) *If a man vow a vow unto the Lord, or swear an oath to bind his soul with a bond, he shall not break his word; he shall do according to all that proceedeth out of his mouth.* Upon which words St. Augustin says, (Q. 56, in Numb.) *He that voweth abstinence from a thing lawful, maketh it unlawful to himself by the vow.* St. Paul gave the example of continency in his own person, and recommends it to the Laity in general; *but I speak this by council,* (κατα συγγνωμην) *not by Commandment.* (1 Cor. vii. 6.) *For I would that all men were even as I myself.*

This, Sir, since you give me such patient attention, reminds me of another great difference, which exists between the Church of England, and the Church of Rome. By the XIIIth *Article of your Religion, you hold that works done before the Grace of Christ and the inspiration of his spirit, are not pleasant to God, for as much as they spring not of faith in Jesus Christ they have the nature of sin.* And by the XIVth Article of your Religion *you further believe, that voluntary works besides, over and above God's Commandments, which they call Acts of Supererogation, cannot be taught without arrogance*

gance and impiety. We, Sir, on the contrary, believe that all actions, which are morally good, or, perhaps of themselves indifferent, may be performed without being in the slightest degree sinful; for nothing but the actual malice of the heart can affix any degree of sin to the natural action. We make a standing difference between the Commandments of Almighty God, and many other good and virtuous actions, which we are counselled, but not commanded to perform. We believe that the observance of the Commandments alone is sufficient to entitle us to everlasting happiness in Heaven, but that the Evangelical counsels are additional helps and means for attaining that end, the least of which shall not loose its reward according to that, (Mat. x. 42.) *Whosoever shall give to drink unto one of these little ones, a cup of cold water only, in the name of a Disciple, Verily I say unto you, he shall in no wise loose his reward.* There are particular passages in Saint Paul, in which he strongly marks out the difference between the Evangelical Precepts and Counsel; for instance, where he recommends the state of virginity in preference to the married state. (1 Cor. vii. 25.) *Now concerning virgins I have no Commandment of the Lord; yet I give my judgment.* (38.) *He that giveth her in marriage doeth well, but he that giveth her not in marriage doeth better.*

The history of the young man in the Gospel will explain our doctrine more explicitly and minutely than any reason or observation whatsoever. (Mark, x. 17.) *And when he was gone forth into the way, there came one running, and kneeled to him, and asked him, Good Master, what shall I do that I may inherit eternal life?* Our Blessed Lord enumerated then the Commandments unto him, and the young man replied, that he had observed them from his youth; *then Jesus beholding him, loved him.* Here you see that the observance of the Commandments entitled him to eternal life, and procured for him the favour and love of Almighty God. He had observed all that had been commanded him, whatever then he could do *besides, and over and above these Commandments,* was an act of supererogation. Yet Jesus Christ loving him, would give him a particular call to greater perfection, by following the Evangelical counsels of voluntary poverty and mortification, and at the same time promises him an extraordinary reward in Heaven, if he embraces this voluntary life of self-abnegation. *And Jesus said unto him, one thing thou lackest; go thy way, sell whatsoever thou hast, and give to the poor, and thou shalt have treasure in Heaven, and come take up the cross, and follow me* No man will seriously advance, that this total renunciation

tion of earthly wealth is a precept or Commandment of God; if it is, then no person dying possessed of any worldly fortune whatever can be saved, for, to *inherit eternal life, we must keep the Commandments.* (James xi. 10.) *For whosoever shall keep the whole law, and yet offend in one point, he is guilty of all.* It was then something more *than is of bounden duty required*, or an act of supererogation; and yet, Jesus Christ does not condemn the young man of arrogance and impiety, *for doing voluntary works, besides over and above God's Commandments,* but expresly promises him *treasure in Heaven* for doing them; but treasure in Heaven is not the reward of arrogance and impiety; so the Roman Catholic Church teaches, that such acts of supererogation are very acceptable and agreeable to Almighty God, and meritorious to ourselves, that is, by the performance of them in the state of Grace, we may gain particular reward or treasure in Heaven.

This brings into my mind, the weight of of scandal, which is taken at the Roman Catholic's doctrine of *merit*, which is seldom, if ever, understood by our adversaries, as believed and taught by ourselves. We believe that no action done by the natural free will of man, as it is the work of man, can deserve or acquire any reward in Heaven. No action performed by a soul in the

state of mortal sin, can possibly be meritorious, or deserve *treasure* in Heaven: for that purpose we must be like the young man in the Gospel, in the state of grace, that is, in the observance of all the Commandments. Our belief then is, *First*, That those works only are meritorious, which are done by a soul, dignified with the grace of God inherent in her, and the value of this action, making it meritorious, proceeds from this grace of God which is in every soul that is in the state of grace. *Secondly*, That no person can perform any such meritorious action without the actual grace of God exciting him thereunto. *Thirdly*, That the grace of God, must be aiding and assisting him all the time, during which he is performing any such meritorious action. (Con. Trid. Sess. vi. c. xvi.) We add moreover, that even to such actions done in this manner, Almighty God is not obliged to give any such reward: but he was pleased to promise and give this Heavenly reward out of his free gracious goodness, he being moved by the merits and passions of Christ, from which all the aforesaid graces flow, to accept for his sake all those works as rewardable: such works being by his grace made worthy to be accepted of, so as to be recompenced by that Heavenly reward, which God hath mercifully promised to them. In this sense alone, we understand
all

all those texts of Scripture, which promise treasure in Heaven, as the reward, hire or wages of good actions. (Mat. v. 12.) *Rejoice and be exceeding glad; for great is your reward in Heaven.* (Mat. xvi. 27.) *He shall reward every man according to his works.* He says not according to his mercy, but according to our works. (Mat. xix. 27.) *We have forsaken all and followed thee; what shall we have therefore?* Here is an act o supererogation, for which Saint Peter, in the name of the other Apostles, asks what will be the reward. Jesus Christ does not however charge them with arrogance or impiety; but tells them that they shall *sit upon twelve thrones, judging the twelve Tribes of Israel, and shall receive an hundred fold, and shall inherit everlasting life.*

The Roman Catholic Church moreover teaches, that these voluntary acts of piety, when performed by persons in the state of grace, have a great satisfactory virtue, by which the pain due to our sins is forgiven, and is more or less cancelled, as the works are more or less perfect. For we teach, that after the sin itself is forgiven, by our true repentance and humble confession, there yet remains the guilt of temporal pain, to which that sin makes us still liable. This naturally leads into another part of our doctrine, concerning *Purgatory* and *Prayers for the dead*, which has been grossly misrepresented

represented and highly abused by our religious antagonists.

The ground of the doctrine is this, that there are some sins, of a slighter nature, which are not deserving of Hell torments; for which, however, we must satisfy by voluntary good works in this life, or by temporary punishments in the next life. For, as we know that nothing defiled shall enter into the Kingdom of Heaven, so we believe, that the soul cannot contract even the slightest stain of sin, (except the original sin in which we are all born) but by her own voluntary motion and consent. Consequently, that she cannot purge herself in this world of it, but by her voluntary repentance and satisfaction ; for we believe, that the merits of Jesus Christ are not applied to us, (except in the sacrament of infant baptism) but by our own means and co-operation. Believing therefore, that there is a place of punishment after this life, where the soul is to satisfy for such sins, for which she shall not have fully satisfied in this life: that such souls, even under this purgation of torment, are a part of the Church of Christ which is intitled to eternal life; and that they have a communication with the prayers of the Church Militant upon earth: we maintain that Almighty God both can and will, for the sake of the good works performed here on earth by his
servants

servants in the state of grace, and by them for that purpose applied to the merits of Jesus Christ, take off or shorten the pains of those souls, who are in this purging place of torment.

If the *doctrine of Purgatory be as you say,* (Art. xii.) *a fond thing vainly invented, and grounded upon no warranty of Scripture, but rather repugnant to the word of God,* whence then did it gain so early and general an admission into the Church of God? Although you reject the books of the Maccabees as Apocrypha, yet by the third Council of Carthage, holden in the year of our Lord 397, they are registered in the Canon: and your Church reads them *for example of life and instruction of manners* (Art. vi.) which it would not certainly do, if they did not contain true and authentic history, (2. Mac. xii. 43.) *He making a gathering, sent twelve thousand drachms of silver to Jerusalem, to have sacrifice offered for the sins of the dead; well and righteously thinking of the resurrection. For unless he hoped, that they, who were slain should rise again, it should seem superfluous and vain to pray for the dead. It is therefore a holy and healthful cogitation to pray for the dead, that they may be loosed from their sins.* Hence it appears, that two hundred years before the coming of Christ, at a time when God's chosen people served him with much

fervor

fervor and sincerity; their High Priest Judas Macchabeus, a man of respectable and holy character, together with all the people, believed that prayers for the dead were laudable and profitable; and that it was then, (as it is to this day) the practice of the Jewish Church to pray for the dead. The practice of antiquity in the Christian Church and the testimony of all the Holy Fathers universally, go to establish this doctrine, and prove the actual usage to have immemorially existed in the Church of Christ.

To say that purgatory is not warranted by Scripture, because the word is no where to be found in Scripture, is an argument which would annihilate our faith in the blessed Trinity, because the word *Trinity* is no where mentioned in the Holy Scriptures. There are numberless instances, in which the Scriptures distinguish between greater and less sins, and the respective punishments due to each. (Mat. v. 22.) *Whoever is angry with his brother without a cause, shall be in danger of the judgment; and whosoever shall say to his brother, Raca, shall be in danger of the council; but whosoever shall say, thou fool, shall be in danger of Hell fire.* Whence it is evident, that there are some offences, which shall be punished by Almighty God, yet not in Hell flames: and it is plain, that he speaks of the punishments of the next life, by mentioning *Hell fire*.

There

There are several texts in the New Testament, which the Roman Catholic Church understands immediately of Purgatory and praying for the dead. (1. Cor. xv. 29.) *Else what shall they do, who are baptized for the dead, if the dead rise not at all? Why are they then baptized for the dead?* Saint Hierom, Basil, Bede, and others, understand these words of the baptism, or cleansing of pennance: and so also do they expound those words of (Mat. iii. 11.) *he shall baptize you with the Holy Ghost and with fire:* that is to say, with the Holy Ghost, or sanctifying grace in this world, and with fire in the next world; nor can they mean Hell Fire, for that does not wash away, cleanse, or baptize, but only punishes and torments: Saint Gregory Nazianzen, expressly calls the fire of purgatory, *the last baptism.* The same and all the other fathers of the Church understand this purgatory, by that place of satisfaction spoken of (Mat. v. 26.) *Thou shalt by no means come out thence, till thou hast paid the utmost farthing.* Upon which Saint Hierom expressly saith, *Thou shalt not go out of prison till thou shalt pay even to thy little sins.*

We moreover conclude from those words of (St. Mat. xii. 32.) *It shall not be forgiven him, either in this world, or in the world to come,* that some sins may be remitted in the next world: but neither in Heaven or in Hell: for sin cannot enter the former, or be released from the latter. In a word, I shall close this point, with the interpretation, which Saint Ambrose gives to the words of Saint Paul, (1 Cor. iii. 15.) *If any man's works shall be burnt, he shall suffer less; but he himself shall be saved; yet so as by fire, Whereas,* saith this Holy Father, (Serm. 20. in Psalm 118.) *Saint Paul saith, yet so as by fire, he sheweth indeed, that he shall be saved, but yet shall suffer the punishment of fire; that being purged by fire, he may be saved and not tormented for ever, as Infidels are by everlasting fire.*

Since you have, Sir, honoured me with such constant attention, I will trespass, but some few minutes longer, upon your good nature. I am sensible, that the strongest prepossessions have engaged the minds of most Protestants, against the Roman Catholic doctrine of indulgences; but, I am free to say, that their prejudice arises from the misconception, not from the extravagancy of the tenet. You will be pleased to throw back your attention to what I have before said; you will then reflect, that after the actual forgiveness of sin, there often remains a temporal satisfaction, which Almighty God requires of the penitent, and which must be complied with, either in this world, or in the next; and further that Jesus Christ gave to the head or chief pastor of his
Church

Church (Mat. xvi. 19.) *the keys of the Kingdom of Heaven.* For though the power of *loosing and binding,* was afterwards given to the other Apostles. (John xx. 23.) Yet, *the keys of the Kingdom of Heaven,* are never in Scripture said to be given to any, but Saint Peter.

An *indulgence* does not at all consist in the forgiveness of sin, much less in the permission to commit it with impunity, as many have through ignorance or malice asserted. Our faith teaches us, that no power on earth, can forgive one mortal or venial offence, without a true contrition, or due sorrow in the sacrament of penance on our part, always to be accompanied with a sincere purpose of offending no more. All that is forgiven by an indulgence, is the whole or part of that temporal pain, or satisfaction, which yet, according to God's justice, we stand liable to pay for the sin already forgiven.

The first requisite (without which there is no possibility of obtaining an indulgence) is to have true faith, producing true repentance for our sins,—this is going further than you ever require, for by (XI. Article of Religion) you hold, *that you are justified by faith only, and not for your own works or deservings.* We Roman Catholics believe, that faith *only working by Charity,* will justify according to that of St. Paul, (1 Cor. xiii. 2.)

xiii. 2.) *And though I have all faith, so that I could remove mountains, and have not charity, I am nothing;* but St. James more expresly delivers our doctrine in the (2 chap. of his Epistle, ver. 14.) *What doth it profit, my brethren, though a man say, he have faith, and have not works? Can faith save him?* (ver. 17.) *Even so faith, if it hath not works is dead, being alone.* (ver. 19.) *Thou believest that there is one God, thou doest well; the Devils also believe and tremble. But wilt thou know, O vain man, that faith without works is dead.* (ver. 24.) *You see then, how that by works a man is justified, and not by faith only.* By your rule of faith, the very instant a sinner hath faith, he is justified; we, following the doctrine of the Apostle, maintain such faith to be dead without works: and that man is not justified till his faith hath produced good works, the first of which is repentance; even after this, we further require him, 1st. To make an entire and true confession of all his grievous sins. 2dly. To make perfect restitution of every thing, to which he is bound. 3dly. To perform faithfully the penance enjoined. 4thly. If this penance fall short of satisfying the Divine Justice, for the pains yet due to the sins forgiven, the sinner stands still obliged to satisfy the Divine Justice by further penal works.

Now

Now all that our Church ever taught concerning indulgences, is, that by an indulgence the whole or part of this pain may be pardoned or remitted, and not even that, by indulgences granted merely at the Pope's pleasure, but by such only, to which the performance of certain virtuous actions are annexed; so that in fact, an indulgence is only an anticipated remission of future penalties after death, which are necessary towards satisfying the Divine Justice for our sins, by commutation of other good works, such as prayers, alms, deeds, fasting, &c, which for that purpose we voluntarily undertake in this life. It is not possible then that this doctrine of the Roman Catholic Church should in any sense encourage, countenance, or permit the commission of sin; for long before a Christian can obtain an indulgence, he must do that, which your Church holds to be alone necessary for his justification, and all that, which we require over and above, is, that he do something more to satisfy the Divine Justice for his sins.

This, Sir, is the real state of the Roman Catholic doctrine, which by the grace of Almighty God I shall ever be ready to seal by my oath, or with my blood, if called upon to do it; and I will venture to say as much of every one of my own Church who knows and practises his own religion. I have not really endeavoured to deceive or mislead

mislead you, though you may have often heard, that we may lawfully break our faith, promises, and even oaths, made to Heretics for the advancement of our own religion. From what I have before said, you will perceive that it is scarcely possible that one individual should be able to condemn another of heresy; we hold and believe, as I suppose you also do, that an oath or promise to do what is sinful, is itself one sin, and to perform the sinful condition of such sinful oath or promise, is also another sin. Now we never taught, or were even maliciously said to teach, that it was sinful to make an oath or promise to any person of any description in the whole world, and it is, and always has been the doctrine of our Church, that the breach of every oath or promise of a thing lawful, is unlawful and sinful; but as for our practice, I appeal to your own sense, experience in life, and knowledge of mankind, to determine what that has ever been, and still is in this particular. In affairs between man and man, even upon life and death, *our* oaths are admitted to be of equal weight and obligation as *your* oaths: this could not be, if we held it not only inoffensive, but even laudable, to *break faith with Heretics*, and if we did really maintain this doctrine, what consideration or motive could possibly withhold us from the sweets, charms, and allurements

allurements of wealth, honour, and power, which the conſtitution opens indifferently to thoſe, who ſubſcribe to the oaths propoſed by government.

 I muſt now take my leave of you, Sir, and I truſt that in our next interview, you may poſſibly think the body of Roman Catholics do not deſerve that exceſs of rigour and perſecution, to which the law now ſubjects them.

F I N I S.

www.ingramcontent.com/pod-product-compliance
Lightning Source LLC
Chambersburg PA
CBHW030407170426
43202CB00010B/1524